The Last Generation

The Last Generation

prose and
poetry

by Cherríe
Moraga

South End Press   Boston, MA

Cover art, "Mis Madres" ©1986 by Estér Hernández.
All rights reserved.
Cover design by Nancy Adams. Page design by the South End
Press collective.
Back cover photo ©1993 by Jean Weisinger.
Some of this work previously appeared in: *The Chicano Codi-
ces* (The Mexican Museum, 1992), *Chicana Lesbians: The Girls Our
Mothers Warned Us About* (Third Woman Press, 1991), *The Irvine
Chicano Literary Prize* (University of California at Irvine, 1988), *An
Ear to the Ground: New American Poetry* (University of Georgia
Press, 1989), *Quarry West, ZYZZYVA, The Berkeley Poetry Review*,
Frontiers: A Journal of Women's Studies, and *Matrix*.

Library of Congress Cataloging-in-Publication Data
Moraga, Cherríe.
The last generation/ Cherríe Moraga.
p.cm.
Includes bibliographical references.
ISBN 0-89608-467-1: $30.00.--ISBN 0-89608-466-3: $14.00
1. Mexican Americans--Literary collections. 2. Mexican
Americans. I.Title.
PS3563.0753L371993
813'.54--dc20

                                                             93-703
                                                             CIP
South End Press, 116 Saint Botolph Street, Boston, MA 02115
99 98 97 96 95 94 93   1 2 3 4 5 6 7 8

Contents

Agradecimientos to all my colegas, comadres, y camaradas who provided me with the support, advice, and inspiration to complete this book, especially Yvonne Yarbro-Bejarano, Myrtha Chabrán, Ellen Gavin, and Ricardo Bracho. Also, thanks to Cathy Arellano for her computer skills.

Some names have been changed
to protect the innocent.

Debe haber otro modo...
Otro modo de ser humano y libre
Otro modo de ser.
— Rosario Castellanos

To honor the legacies of
Audre Lorde and César Chávez.

For the yet unborn.

Introduction

"Pray for others." This is what the elders taught her.
"Praying for yourself is only one prayer."

$\mathbf{T}$*he Last Generation* is written as a prayer at a time when I
no longer remember how to pray. I complete this book 500 years
after the arrival of Cristóbal Colón. Its publication reflects a minor
Mexican moment in an otherwise indifferent world literary history.
Colón's accidental arrival to these lands, on the other hand, was an
event of catastrophic consequence to the world, literary and otherwise. Still, in my mind, the two events are somehow intimately

connected—the violent collision between the European and the Indigenous, the birth of a *colon*ization that would give birth to me.

In 1524, just three years after the Spanish Conquest of the Aztec Empire, the Náhuatl sages, the tlamatinime, came before the missionary friars in defense of their religion. "Our gods are already dead," they stated. "Let us perish now." Their codices lay smoldering in heaps of ash.

I write with the same knowledge, the same sadness, recognizing the full impact of the colonial "experiment" on the lives of Chicanos, mestizos, and Native Americans. Our codices—dead leaves unwritten—lie smoldering in the ashes of disregard, censure, and erasure. *The Last Generation* emerges from those ashes. I write it against time, out of a sense of urgency that Chicanos are a disappearing tribe, out of a sense of this disappearance in my own familia.

At my fortieth birthday party, my tíos and tías sit talking around the dinner table. Most are in their late seventies now, and I notice their whitening hair and frail bodies, their untiring dignity. I relish the sound of their elegant and common Spanish, the subtlety of their humor and vividness of their recovered memories, their cuentos. Watching them, I know lo mexicano will die with their passing. My tíos' children have not taught their own children to be Mexicans. They have become "Americans." And we're all supposed to quietly accept this passing, this slow and painless death of a cultura, this invisible disappearance of a people. But I do not accept it. I write. I write as I always have, but now I write for a much larger familia.

.....

The poems here span a period of about seven years, beginning with my return to Aztlán in 1985 from a five-year self-imposed exile in the Northeast. The essays are all relatively recent, written within the first three years of this decade, beginning with the loss of the Sandinista election in early 1990 and ending with the Quincentenary in 1992. After a long period of silence, I had imagined I had given up the essay, until the political urgency of the times—the Gulf War, the collapse of the Soviet Union, Indigenous peoples' international campaigns for sovereignty, the hundreds of thousands of deaths of gay people, women, and people of color from AIDS and breast cancer, the Los Angeles Rebellion, and the blatant refusal by the United States to commit to environmental protection at the Earth Summit in Brazil—called me to respond.

History is "advancing" at an unprecedented speed. A writer-friend tells me, "Everything we write nowadays is outdated before we've finished." I have to agree. Still, history is always stumbling, always limping a few steps behind prophecy. And it is prophecy that drives this writing—not my personal prophecy, but the prophecy of a people.

The date is October 17, 1989. I am returning home from work, traveling across the Bay Bridge. The Union Oil 76 sign reads 4:53 pm. My eyes scan the city skyline, ever amazed at its growing enormity, and then I think, in seconds, the whole thing could go...*I don't know why I think this, but eleven minutes later, pulling into my neighborhood, a seven-point earthquake shakes the Bay Area.*

It's all just a sign of the times and every writer is a prophet if she only opens her heart and listens. The journey of this writing is as much a journey into the past as it is into the future, a resurrection of the ancient in order to construct the modern. It is that place where prophecy and past meet and speak to each other. Although I cannot pretend their wisdom, I see my task as that of the ancient Mesoamerican scribes: to speak to these cataclysmic times, to expose the "dream world" of individualism, profit, and consumerism. Truth must be expressed in "Flower and Song," the sages professed. In metaphor. So these are not essays as much as they are poems and these are not poems as much as they are essays. Possibly the distinction no longer matters—between the poem and the essay, between my art and activism. As Audre Lorde wrote, "Poetry is not a luxury. It is a vital necessity of our existence." This picture book I write is a drawing made of words—sometimes elegant, most times raw, always in earnest. The stories have a lot to do with Chicano culture and Indian people and homosexuals and half-breeds and women loving and hating women. They are a queer mixture of glyphs, these writings, but they shape the world I know at the turn of this century. These final letters are the last marks to be placed in this book and the first pages you will read. Like the ancient codices, *The Last Generation* begins at the end and moves forward.

— December 31, 1992

The Last Generation

I am the space occupying the middle of the sofa. The sofa in the same front room that was off limits to us as children. They, this family of cousins, had a den. Children belonged in the den. (Was the "den" an invention of the fifties?) Front rooms were just that: rooms in the front, never altered by human contact, except on christmas eve when half of the expansive room was filled with a tree, the tip of which always had to be sawed off by my Tío Samuel, the father of the family. The one with the wide belly and the rough hands of a man, a worker, a man who worked with his hands.

We, on the other hand, were not a family like this family because we did not have a father like that father nor a den. We had a father with soft pink hands and a front room that was used every day of the week by everyone in the family. A front room separated from the dining room by an ironing board and two huge sacks of laundry, one of which I remember always contained neatly rolled little burritos of sweet-smelling wet starched cotton.

And there was, of course, the t.v. in its ever-popular pivotal position. All the furniture, whether peopled or not, posed expectantly in view of the tube. "You should be an engineer," my mother would boast. I was the only one in the family who had the required sensitivity and know-how to maintain that perfect balance between channel dial and clothes-hanger antenna, creating a picture with snow kept at a one-inch maximum level. I was also told I should be a chiropractor or a lawyer. The first, when I would straddle my mother's thin hips and press her back to the floor, her wailing in relief. The second, when I began to exhibit the first glimmerings of political consciousness and my protests sent most of the family, with the exception of my ever-faithful big sister, away from the table with indigestion. Vietnam atrocities splattered like red chile over the nopalitos.

But what I really wanted to be was a musician. That was the only other time kids were allowed in my tíos' front room. Piano lessons. Once a week, a stranger in a dark suit who was rumored to have the breath of an old goat came to give my cousins lessons. I couldn't vouch for the breath because the closest I got to him was about ten feet away, when I squeezed myself between the wall and the back of the sofa to get first-hand for free what my cousins were paying for.

Bad breath or not, how I envied those small hands sheltered by the hot weight of the man's as he stretched and coaxed and begged a response from my cousins. But their hands were as dead as lead and mine were itching to fly and sing and dance across that keyboard. So after a few months, my tía said it was like throwing money down the toilet, and the piano stood silent again. Silent and grand. Its lid, a mouth stretched wide wide open ready to sing or moan or howl in rage, but today...

This christmas it appears more bored than anything else, tired of this life and this family. A great black yawn in the corner whose purpose in life has been reduced to providing an extra seat for company on christmas. A new generation of cousins, legs dangling in even descending patterns from its bench: black patent leather, Adidas tennis shoes, white baby high-tops. A sea of christmas wrapping beneath them.

And I am the space occupying the middle of the sofa.

I never became a musician or a lawyer or a chiropractor for that matter. Neither did my cousins. They made babies. And I wonder for a moment about creativity. They created babies. But when? When was the act of creation? At conception? At the moment of impregnation? During the hours spent in labor waiting for the new life to expel itself? Or is it the daily toil that makes up the creation? Then creativity is the hours spent wiping dirty nalgas, washing and folding laundry, cleaning mocos off forever running noses, changing wet bedding.

I am the space occupying the middle of the sofa. Since I have no children I am worse than an inept musician. My hands have been so busy touching things, getting themselves on as much as fast as they could, that I have nothing to show for my life. No babies. No little feet dangling from the piano bench with just my curl of baby toe, like my father's.

I am disappearing into this couch. I envy them, my cousins— the men—and their trim morena wives: patient, pregnant, steadily middle-class, and climbing...to what? Their almond-eyed children who will never hear from their parents' mouths the meaning/memory of that chata face, that high rooster'd chest. But my tío remembers, and tells me, the sponge, the childless timeless one, everything. Cornering me:

"We were the Indians that built the San Gabriel Mission."

"I thought you were all dead," I say.

"It was all our land," he continues. "This entire valle. We owned from..."

I barely reach his belly (that's the kind of Indian I am) and I bend my neck way back to take in the whole breadth of him and his pride compressed into these three minutes we share in the hallway waiting for the bathroom.

"Where did Ceci go?" I hear my sister call from the kitchen. I am now in the den where most of the viejos are, including my orphan father. The one who stole the Mission from the Spanish (and from the Indians enslaved by the Spanish) without a dime to show for it.

Rebecca is doing a little dance. She is my father's granddaughter. There is no sign of her grandmother, la Mexicana, having entered the picture. The grandchildren, they're the ones who turn up with the grandfather's eyes, a pale blue in a flurry of light lashes. Rebecca has wrapped herself in her mother's red wool scarf and is performing a two-and-a-half-year-old version of Jingle Bells for her tamales-fed, sleepy-from-too-much-kids-and-beer captive audience. My Dad lays a heavy arm around my shoulder. "She sure is somethin'. Isn't she, daughter? " Yeah, Dad. She sure is.

"Clap!" My niece commands. "Clap!" And we all comply, me and this brood of spouses the women in my family have taken on. All good men. Quiet men. They accept my presence among them because I am without a man but old enough to have known a few. And I feel just like the piano in the next room, a great big yawn in the middle of the sofa.

My family is beginning to feel its disintegration. Our Mexican grandmother of ninety-six years has been dead two years now and la familia's beginning to go. Ignoring this, it increases in number. I am the only one who doesn't ignore this because I am the only one not contributing to the population. My line of family stops with me. There will be no one calling me, *Mami, Mamá, Abuelita...*

I am the last generation put on this planet to remember and record.

No one ever said to me, you should be a writer some day. But I went ahead and did it anyway. Like most things, I went ahead and did it.

– christmas eve, 1986

New Mexican
Confession

En Route para Los Angeles

After awhile it comes down to a question
of life choices not a choice between you/or her
this sea town/or that bruising city
but about putting one foot in front of the other
and ending up somewhere
that looks like home.

Salinas is not my home,
although the name is right
and the slow curve of road 'round the fence
where farmworker buses are kept imprisoned overnight
outhouses trailing
stinking after them.

I am always en route *through* that town,
but managed five years en Nueva York
where the name doesn't sound right
even spanglicized
it's cold yanqui blue bruised.

Your body couldn't be the land
only made me want it more
'cause indoors everything could be México
if I closed my eyes and imagined

the hot breath beneath the blankets in winter
rivers of apartment sweat in summer
was that country I had abandoned
with my womanhood awakened.

ii.
On the grapevine of the interstate
I first turned my back on my los angeles
my head to a future miss america/mexican
legacy.

Now I return
nodding off a greyhound
dreaming of you and the trail
of small deaths behind me.

Are you a dreamer, too?

It is a kind of dying, this parting
one we imagine freely chosen
in the way one chooses a wife
how far a part
to space the children.

iii.
Nightly before I left you
I dreamed of dying
not my own, but others loved
and abandoned.

Figured it the woman I beat dust tracks to find,
figured *that* lover covered in wounds
was calling me in my sleep.

But it was you
running through my cupped palms
as I brought you to my lips you
I mourned with the dead you
never get a chance to say good bye.

I thought some body some where
wants me to get wind of this
que el camino real is full
of these rude awakenings
unto death.

They Was Girls Together

For Vienna

It was a poem
that curled the girls'
knuckles 'round
chainlink
white bone splitting
through clenched brown
fists. It was
a poem

that held the two women
in the grip
of a rhetoric they found
both their grown mouths shaping
with voices thin
as november air.

"I thought you had my back!"
It was
a poem

that enveloped
their tiny brooklyn-blocked world
made love to their innocence
and fresh sharp-stabbed
sense of betrayal.

They was girls together *
trying to do the impossible:
love.

It was a poem
that forgave them

their failure.

*Toni Morrison's *Sula.*

The Ecology of Woman

Why hold a grudge against a place, a country?
— The Mixquiahuala Letters

1. Mexico City, 1985.

The room is huge. Three double beds. Slow season in la capital. Rain.

Once friends filled the room momentarily. Not exactly friends, but faces she recognized, faces that spoke a language whose signs she'd learned to interpret through years of northern city dwelling. Each a sponge holding in her liquid balm. One with a weight familiar

to her weight she let fall fully down on top of her and slept a deep
night's dream under such a cobija.

Cobija. Necesito más cobijas.
She looked up the word in advance to get the right thing, the
singularly exact thing she needed, *más cobijas. Estoy enferma tengo
calentura y un frío...Señora, por favor, ¿me trae más cobijas?*

The hotel maid con la cara de su Tía Pancha brings the girl a thin
blanket from the hall closet, a serape frayed all around its edges, she
crawls under, drawing it up to her chin along with three bedspreads
stripped naked from their springs in the damp of the evening.

So ashamed to be ill before Doña Pancha, Pancha is not her
mother, but pities the young woman *pobrecita niña viajando sola*
through the same eyes that see the girl's skin a stone grey-white like
the sheets she's washed of too many souls wrestling with the
pesadillas of the loveless.

But Cecilia has gone this far to keep her illness to herself, to
be away from the mother. This far to a country where there are no
longer *living* relatives, only dead relics of a past she imagines to
bring her succor. *Socorro.* Virgins of minitature dimension who
weep real tears for daughters wedded to the miseria birthed by the
hungry mouths between their legs.

.....

Days later. Midnight window moon. Cecilia shuns the mirror
of all those she has ever seen naked. She won't think of them here.

She blows out the shape of each one's name on the face of the glass and their reflection clouds as the smog of the city settles into a frozen stillness overnight.

Still México does offer a mirror of sorts. Put up to her face, it plays back the amusement park version. Her flesh distorted into proportions impossible to inhabit: *güera / norteamericana / pocha / gringa / turista / hembra / sola / hembra / huérfana /* hembrahembrahembra...

2. *Zihuatanejo*

I let him touch my nipple I don't know why I let him sit by me on that beach and gently stroke my right nipple back and forth back and forth with no clear purpose except he wanted to make love and as I hadn't in ten years with a man and I was lonely to put something solid between my legs I let him stroke my nipple back and forth back and forth hardening...

—Halo. Te vi ayer. Siempre he tenido, no sé por qué, desde que era niño...una atracción por las mujeres vellosas—for this was foreplay, after all, though it would be hours before he'd disappoint her with his body.

When it is over, the boy will walk her to a corner to catch a cab. —Nos vemos mañana en la playa—he says and she slams the door against the prospect, already knowing morning will find her bags packed, leaving the shape of that boy, she would like to have reduced her own abundant body into its neat contour of high breast bone, flat belly, lean hips, tucked smugly into bathing suit covertly coveting his secret.

But there is no secret. With soundless drop, all is revealed, no subtlety of suggestion. No wonder. Except his.
—¿Es que 'stas casada?
—No.
—¿Tienes novio?
—No.
—¿Vives con alguien?
—No. No. No.
—Bueno. Es que te gustan las mujeres. Dicen que a las mujeres muy vellosas les gustan las mujeres.

And she remembers where she is. México. After the revolution.

For a moment she sees herself as he sees the body that refuses a lean line, the circle of independent unruly strands stroking each nipple, the eruption of coarse dark wires flooding the swell of her belly, the fur that coats her legs from thigh to ankle glistening gold from so much sol y brisa salada.

Sí, soy una mujer velluda.
Sí, soy.
Y a mí me gustan las mujeres.

That night she heads back to her hotel, walking the beach alone. Men with rifles and uniforms sit on rocks comtemplando el mar and the decent job they got. It was worth the trek over las sierras where primos pick at the dirt for a root. Here they guard turistas from unwanted guests like the boy whose scent she still carries.

I am a woman walking the beach solita.

She suspects they know where she's been. They decide her fate: otra gringa who will give it up *por nada.* They exchange glances, the soldier and she exchange words, a few. She is lonely and longs for the good conversation of a woman.

He has a gun he really has a gun
not just in his pocket
but over his shoulder.

She walks on holding her back stiff against the barrel placed there.

Although she showered with the boy, she does so again, stretching across cool hotel sheets. The fan overhead lapping gusts of tepid air, sponging water from her flesh. She is oddly satiated, though he never gave her the satisfaction of having to do nothing but throw back her hands and scream. No, she was different. The touch of her hand too confident in its fingered hold of ribcage, its square grasp of thigh and buckling buttocks. These were the hands of a woman who took charge, so he rolled onto his back and she rode him as she did all those lazy cowboys of her past.

After removing the evidence of the boy, she allows the pleasure of the company of women in her dream of the child she'll have. It is a girl, a daughter to be sure. She imagines the tender fleshseed growing inside her. The one who will call her mami and forgive her the calling of her own mother's name for the last time.

3. México Returned

When the blood dyes
the sheets red in the bed
of Mexico City
she feels no loss.
It was a dream
awakened.

For three days, she gives birth
to her own motherless
blood.

Hermit's Prayer

if I were a boy like him
I would cloak myself in monks' robes
protected from crimes of passion
I would not be expected to love
to heal with my hands
my kiss
my voice
to bleed
I would not be expected to bleed.

Lyfe Cycle

el inocente
animalito that he is
spies the german shepherd
as she plops herself down to piss
on the impatiens
and the urge wells up in him, too
naturally

the grey guzanito
of life sprays a wide arc
into the same dog puddle
bubbles burrowing into the earth
blood scents mixing

his compadrecito
vigilando todo
cuts loose with a laugh
it's a boy's game
their bodies like two young colts
soft down fur stretched over knobby knees
skin glistening in the midday heat

"¿Qué 'stás haciendo? Do you see a toilet here?"

Caught.
the puppy dog eyes widen
roll up into an arc
meeting hers, narrowing

"No."

it's not a faucet he can turn off
still sputtering
the worm ducks its head back
behind the snap of elastic
the red cloth darkening

they teach us to knock
the animal out of them

and as her hips turn against his face
jersey shimmering in the midday heat
she can't help but recall her own
animal girlhood
that once grovelled in the dirt
delighted
in the fecundity
of earth between teeth
that once
sucked the teats
of the same
species who asked
no more
than that she grow
in bone & limb & breath
to one day offer the same
to another
hungry
animal
mouth

Just Vision

Your cosmic or third eye is a synthesis of your two eyes.
Neither left nor right views, just vision.
—El Centro Campesino Cultural,
"Footsteps of the Creator"

I once imagined
my bones and muscles were made
of steel and rotors
and I could do it
stretch/leap/throw myself
across any barrier/obstacle:
Wide and turbulent sea of snapping dragons
Fiery pools of naked uplifted arms, sinners awaiting their
salvation
Ocean stiff and still as mud, pressed flat between two pieces
of city,

just to get to the other side,
just to keep the two halves of my self
from cracking
down
wide
open
through the center of my skull.

But I have seen that mass
of brain and blood, the splitting has already occurred.
There is a faint line of fault

driven like a stake into the spot. Where once was the third eye
seeking both sides to everything
keeping each eye, right and left
from wandering off
too far.

Poema como valentín

(or a San Francisco Love Poem)

An artist friend
once showed me how to see

color as a black & white
phenomenon.

Look. See that broad-faced glistening leaf?
Look. See where it is white, a light
magnet to the sun?
Look. See where it is black?

The eye narrows
into a pinpoint focus
of what was never
green, really
only light condensing
into dark.

You could paint a portrait
this way, seeing
from black to white.

Her mouth would still
be rose and round
but less tired of explaining

itself

and as I pressed mine to it
it could remember no mouth
evenly vaguely reminiscent
no mouth with this particular
blend of wet and warm
in the darkest and fullest
place that sustains me

while all the world of this city weeps
beneath a blanket
of intercepted

light.

Reunion

For my "cousin"

In your oakland apartment
I bring fruta   I remember
the color yellow
of walls, the banana
something else...a flower
the color of a deep rose
yellow, the fine-haired delicacy
of kiwi, we laugh at their tender
resemblance to testicles,
never touched our ruby lips
except sliced with strawberry
sour green
apple

you cut with efficiency.
I watch
the bowl of fruit shrink
between us
silver spoons colliding
we shovel out the remains
I faintly remember
your apology
vaguely recall
a reference to a past

where we parted
ways
I don't remember
words

only the drive
up to your house
my old neighborhood
that black & white memory.

Dreaming of Other Planets

my vision is small
fixed
to what can be heard
between the ears

the spot
between the eyes
a well-spring
opening
to el mundo grande

relámpago strikes
between the legs
I open against
my will dreaming

of other planets I am
dreaming
of other ways
of seeing

this life.

New Mexican Confession

Upon reading Whitman fifteen years later. Jemez Springs, 1988.

1.
There is great joy in the naming
of things that mean no more
than what they are.
Cottonwood in winter's nakedness,
frozen black skeleton
against red rock canyon walls
converging onto this thin river of water
and human activity:
Los Ojos Bar
Hilltop Hotel and Café
the grain and feed shop.

These were the words denied me in any language:
piñón
cañón
arroyo
except as names on street signs,
growing up in california sprawl,
boundaries formed
by neat cement right angles.

2.
Like a poet
I have come here to look for god

but make no claim of finding—
the quest, a journey
of righteous and humble men
strangers to their bodies
cartographers to the contour of woman-flesh,
a border between nature and its lover,
man.

I am a woman
who walks by the motherhouse
of the sisters of the precious blood
sleeping beneath the snow
and can as easily see myself there
my body sleeping beneath the silent
smell of fresh pressed linen,
the protection of closed doors
Against the cold
Against the foul breath 'n' beer
talk of Alaskan pipeliners passing through
Against the vibrant death this land is seeing...

Who do they pray for? Do they pray for this land?

The sister ventures out into the cold of noon
to play the campanas. They sound of tin,
a flat resonance as I pass
not even twelve strikes but a sporadic three strikes here
another two—rest—again three
and I imagine she calls me as I always feared
to join her in her single bed

of aching abstinence.

I am the nun
as I am the Giusewa woman
across the road
who 300 years ago
with mud and straw and hands
as delicate as her descendant's
now scribbling on dead leaves,
walled up the Spanish religion
built templos to enclose his god
while the outer cañón
enveloped and pitied them all.

3.
My sin has always been to believe
myself man, to sing a song
of *my*self that inhabited everyone.

I fall to sleep contemplating the body of the poet
Whitman at my age, 100 years ago
and see his body knew the same fragility,
the desire to dissolve the parameters of flesh
and bone and blend with the mountain
the blade of grass
the boy.

I *bleed* with the mountain
the blade of grass
the boy

because my body suffers in its womb.
The maternal blood that courses this frozen ground
was not spilt in violence, but in mourning.

I am everyman more than man.
This is my sin.
This knowledge.

War Cry

Ni for El Salvador

February 1990

I am a woman nearing forty without children.
I am an artist nearing forty without community.
I am a lesbian nearing forty without partner.
I am a Chicana nearing forty without country.

And if it were safe, I'd spread open my thighs
and let the whole world in
and birth and birth and birth life.
The dissolution of self, the dissolution of borders.

But it is not safe.
Ni for me.
Ni for El Salvador.

So we resist and in resistance, hope is born. An art conceived in hope. Dreams die, crush and die. I have known the death of a love that I had once believed would ferment a revolution. I still seek that love, that woman writer in me who is worth her salt, who is relentlessly hopeful, who can create a theatre, a poetry, a song that dares to expose that very human weakness where we betray ourselves, our loved ones, even our own revolution.

War Cry

lo que quiero es
tierra
si no tierra, pueblo
si no pueblo, amante
si no amante, niño
si no niño
soledad
tranquilidad
muerte

tierra.

Foreign Tongue

She witholds
the language
not the words
but the abandon
they evoke.

She refuses
bites her lip
to repel
el deseo
que quiere
estallar
por la boca.

Traidora
que soy
to discover
la fuerza
de la lengua
por los labios
of another

not hers.

We Have Read a Lot and Know
We Are Not Safe

Oakland, Califas, 1988

A black and white film is our love-making
foreign very serious subtitled.

I can barely discern your face
between the venetian blind slats
of evening streetlamp particled air
piercing this womb of bed and nightstand
half-drunk cups of coffee magazines books
curled into the shape of palms.

You fold back the page of print,
tuck the sheet around my thighs
"But this is not Nicaragua," you tell me.
Still, it is some other place
where we've learned to fear
for our lives.

.....

In this dark movie
where we find ourselves
touching
the thin shield of my flesh hardens
against the tumult, quiet revolution

you pronounce in language
coded for my comprehension...

"You are not so different from anyone else,"
and I don't understand your meaning
and I do

y me ofreces el pecho to the daughter
to give the mother pleasure
to give the daughter courage
and I know we are children y ancianas at once
and this is not a game we play with each other.

We are here to help the other
change and survive
amid the gunshot blasts
outside our iron-barred window.

Tonight there is no peace in each other's arms,
sometimes there is but tonight...
tonight we make love against the darkness
a delicate-fingered ritual of discovery—

Can I stir her back to life
with so much death surrounding us?

The War Continues

Flesh is full
of holes.

It is made
to breathe
secrete
receive.

It is nothing
against
bombs
and
bullets.

It is not meant
to be a barrier
against
anything.

But this dark flesh
will resist you flee
you who believe
you are not made
of the same
skin
and
bones.

La Despedida

In pilgrimage to El Santuario de Chimayó, Nuevo México.

El Sanctuario de Chimayó is a shrine dedicated to "Our Lord of Esquípulas," a large dark figure of the crucified christ, whose Indian origins can be traced to the same santo in Guatemala. Pilgrims visit the shrine daily with supplications. In the back of the church is a candlelit womb-shaped chamber. There is hole in the floor in the center of the chamber. From there supplicants dig out a rich red earth that is said to contain great curative powers.

1. Chimayó

I am not a believer
only a seeker of the spirit
as manifested in acts of MAN,
cynical of all that is not holy
grasped between bleeding palms
burning crosses
tortured tongues of muted
fire.

I enter, peregrina
this stone circle of heat
the *Angel of Death* my companion
not in search of the divine
but of the word made flesh—
retablos that testify

to the miracle of familial love:
"Querido señor, bring mijo home safe."
Vietnam remembered.
Cancerous tumors dissolved.
Broken hearts healed.
The last, my own pitiful wish.

And its earth mouth opens to us...

Soy la santa
five feet of human
dimension and heart.
I birth electric
from the flames of the faithful.
Their burnt offerings singe
my cracked desert lips. Holy water
lágrimas stain my ashen cheeks.

I remember Guatemala and therefore, I weep.

2. Cochita Mesa

Peregrina, I enter her forest
leaves pressing underfoot.
I am riveted by the sight, the *Angel*
of Death before me.
Mirrored in her huge deer eyes
I have neither vagina
nor pigment politicized.
She frightens me in her immense

animalness, such brutal naked strength
outside the law of MAN.

The forest floor supports us
heaves and sighs
beneath our broken
weight.

Tierra bendita
ruega por nosotras
ruega por nosotras
ruega por nosotras.

The dust of her hoof and flight powdering mine...
she is gone.

3. Oakland, Califas

Under your raised arm
I return
to sleep animal cheek against animal breast,
y los angelitos do not sleep with us, protecting
the *Angel of Death,* my nightly companion.

Angelita, remember
that woman you sought
that essence that you could claim, "¡Ya ves!
There she is my beloved, my cecilia, deer-runner girl."
Ya no existe.

True, I once rolled my head
toward that sweet music
your calling my name
ce-ci-i-i-i-i-l-ya
three syllables, one chord
of meaning
spoken with the confidence
that the bearer would indeed turn her face to you
her wondrous moon-like and essentially female
face she would turn the miracle of her
mouth to you and all
that you have ever wanted
would be mirrored in the ageless
animal eyes.

¡Y-A-A-A-A   N-O-O-O-O!

In indian tongue, the word for lonely
is not knowing who you are.
You no longer call my name
and I am no longer
you whom you sought to know.

I remember and therefore I weep.[*]

*Descendants of the Anasazi of Nuevo México.

Proposition

It is very simple
between us
woman to woman
you must leave
to return
again
in another
form
not woman

so we
without fear
of the fathers
can make a country
of our bed.

Art in América con Acento

I write this on the one-week anniversary of the death of the
Nicaraguan Revolution.*

We are told not to think of it as a death, but I am in mourning.
It is an unmistakable feeling. A week ago, the name "Daniel" had
poured from Nicaragüense lips with a warm liquid familiarity. In
private, doubts gripped their bellies and those doubts they took

*An earlier version of this essay first appeared in *Frontiers: A Journal
of Women Studies,* Volume XII, Number 3, University of Colorado, 1992.
It was originally presented as a talk given through the Mexican-American Studies Department at the California State University of Long
Beach on March 7, 1990.

finally to the ballot box. Doubts seeded by bullets and bread: the U.S.-financed Contra War and the economic embargo. Once again an emerging sovereign nation is brought to its knees. A nation on the brink of declaring to the entire world that revolution is the people's choice betrays its own dead. Imperialism makes traitors of us all, makes us weak and tired and hungry.

I don't blame the people of Nicaragua. I blame the U.S. government. I blame my complicity as a citizen in a country that, short of an invasion, stole the Nicaraguan revolution that el pueblo forged with their own blood and bones. After hearing the outcome of the elections, I wanted to flee the United States in shame and despair.

I am Latina, born and raised in the United States. I am a writer. What is my responsibility in this?

.....

Days later, George Bush comes to San Francisco. He arrives at the St. Francis Hotel for a $1,000-a-plate fund raising dinner for Pete Wilson's gubernatorial campaign. There is a protest. We, my camarada and I, get off the subway. I can already hear the voices chanting from a distance. We can't make out what they're saying, but they are Latinos and my heart races, seeing so many brown faces. They hold up a banner. The words are still unclear but as I come closer closer to the circle of my people, I am stunned. "¡Viva la paz en Nicaragua!" it states. "¡Viva George Bush! ¡Viva UNO!" And my heart drops. Across the street, the "resistance" has congregated—less organized, white, young, middle-class students. *¿Dónde 'stá mi pueblo?*

A few months earlier, I was in another country, San Cristóbal, Chiapas, México. The United States had just invaded Panamá. This time, I could stand outside the United States, read the Mexican newspapers for a perspective on the United States that was not monolithic. In the Na Bolom Center Library I wait for a tour of the grounds. The room is filled with norteamericanos. They are huge people, the men slouching in couches. Their thick legs spread across the floor, their women lean into them. They converse. "When we invaded Panama..." I grow rigid at the sound of the word, "we." They are progressives (I know this from their conversation.) They oppose the invasion, but identify with the invaders.

How can I, as a Latina, identify with those who invade Latin American land? George Bush is not my leader. I did not elect him, although my tax dollars pay for the Salvadoran Army's guns. We are a living breathing contradiction, we who live en las entrañas del monstruo, but I refuse to be forced to identify. I am the product of invasion. My father is Anglo; my mother, Mexican. I am the result of the dissolution of blood lines and the theft of language; and yet, I am a testimony to the failure of the United States to wholly anglicize its mestizo citizens.

I wrote in México, "Los Estados Unidos es mi país, pero no es mi patria." I cannot flee the United States, my land resides beneath its borders. We stand on land that was once the country of México. And before any conquistadors staked out political boundaries, this was Indian land and in the deepest sense remains just that: a land sin fronteras. Chicanos with memory like our Indian counterparts recognize that we are a nation within a nation. An internal nation whose existence defies borders of language, geography, race. Chicanos are a multiracial, multilingual people, who since 1848, have been displaced from our ancestral lands or remain upon them as indentured servants to Anglo-American invaders.

Today, nearly a century and a half later, the Anglo invasion of Latin America has extended well beyond the Mexican/American border. When U.S. capital invades a country, its military machinery is quick to follow to protect its interests. This is Panamá, Puerto Rico, Grenada, Guatemala... Ironically, the United States' gradual consumption of Latin America and the Caribbean is bringing the people of the Americas together. What was once largely a chicano/mexicano population in California is now guatemalteco, salvadoreño, nicaragüense. What was largely a Puerto Rican and Dominican "Spanish Harlem" of New York is now populated with Mexicanos playing rancheras and drinking cerveza. This mass emigration is evident from throughout the Third World. Every place the United States has been involved militarily has brought its offspring, its orphans, its homeless, and its casualties to this country: Vietnam, Guatemala, Cambodia, the Philippines...

Third World populations are changing the face of North America. The new face has got that delicate fold in the corner of the eye and that wide-bridged nose. The mouth speaks in double negatives and likes to eat a lot of chile. By the 21st century our whole concept of "America" will be dramatically altered; most significantly by a growing Latino population whose strong cultural ties, economic disenfranchisement, racial visibility, and geographical proximity to Latin America discourages any facile assimilation into Anglo-American society.

Latinos in the United States do not represent a homogenous group. Some of us are native born, whose ancestors precede not only the arrival of the Anglo-American but also of the Spaniard. Most of us are immigrants, economic refugees coming to the United States in search of work. Some of us are political refugees, fleeing death squads and imprisonment; others come fleeing revolution and the loss of wealth. Finally, some have simply landed here very tired of war. And in all cases, our children had no choice in the matter. U.S. Latinos represent the whole spectrum of color and class and political position, including those who firmly believe they can integrate into the mainstream of North American life. The more European the heritage and the higher the class status, the more closely Latinos identify with the powers that be. They vote Republican. They stand under the U.S. flag and applaud George Bush for bringing "peace" to Nicaragua. They hope one day he'll do the same for Cuba, so they can return to their patria and live a "North American-style" consumer life. Because they know in the United States they will never have it all, they will always remain "spics," "greasers," "beaners," and "foreigners" in Anglo-America.

As a Latina artist I can choose to contribute to the development of a docile generation of would-be Republican "Hispanics" loyal to the United States, or to the creation of a force of "disloyal" americanos who subscribe to a multicultural, multilingual, radical re-structuring of América. Revolution is not only won by numbers, but by visionaries, and if artists aren't visionaries, then we have no business doing what we do.

.....

I call myself a Chicana writer. Not a Mexican-American writer, not an Hispanic writer, not a half-breed writer. To be a Chicana is not merely to name one's racial/cultural identity, but also to name a politic, a politic that refuses assimilation into the U.S. mainstream. It acknowledges our mestizaje—Indian, Spanish, and

Africano. After a decade of "hispanicization" (a term superimposed upon us by Reagan-era bureaucrats), the term Chicano assumes even greater radicalism. With the misnomer "Hispanic," Anglo America proffers to the Spanish surnamed the illusion of blending into the "melting pot" like any other white immigrant group. But the Latino is neither wholly immigrant nor wholly white; and here in this country, "Indian" and "dark" don't melt. (Puerto Ricans on the East Coast have been called "Spanish" for decades and it's done little to alter their status on the streets of New York City.)

The generation of Chicano literature being read today sprang forth from a grassroots social and political movement of the sixties and seventies that was definitively anti-assimilationist. It responded to a stated mandate: *art is political*. The proliferation of poesía, cuentos, and teatro that grew out of El Movimiento was supported by Chicano cultural centers and publishing projects throughout the Southwest and in every major urban area where a substantial Chicano population resided. The Flor y Canto poetry festivals of the seventies and a teatro that spilled off flatbed trucks into lettuce fields in the sixties are hallmarks in the history of the Chicano cultural movement. Chicano literature was a literature in dialogue with its community. And as some of us became involved in feminist, gay, and lesbian concerns in the late seventies and early eighties, our literature was forced to expand to reflect the multifaceted nature of the Chicano experience.

The majority of published Chicano writers today are products of that era of activism, but as the Movement grew older and more established, it became neutralized by middle-aged and middle-class concerns, as well as by a growing conservative trend in government. Most of the gains made for farm workers in California were dismantled by a succession of reactionary governors and Reagan/Bush economics. Cultural centers lost funding. Most small press Chicano publishers disappeared as suddenly as they had appeared. What was once a radical and working-class Latino student base on university campuses has become increasingly conservative. A generation of tokenistic affirmative-action policies and bourgeois flight from Central America and the Caribbean has spawned a tiny Latino elite who often turn to their racial/cultural identities not as a source of political empowerment, but of personal employment as tokens in an Anglo-dominated business world.

And the writers...? Today more and more of us insist we are "American" writers (in the North American sense of the word). The body of our literary criticism grows (seemingly at a faster rate than the literature itself), we assume tenured positions in the University, secure New York publishers, and our work moves further and further away from a community-based and national political movement.

.....

A writer will write. With or without a movement.

Fundamentally, I started writing to save my life. Yes, my own life first. I see the same impulse in my students—the dark, the queer, the mixed-blood, the violated—turning to the written page with a relentless passion, a drive to avenge their own silence, invisibility, and erasure as living, innately expressive human beings.

A writer will write with or without a movement; but at the same time, for Chicano, lesbian, gay, and feminist writers—anybody writing against the grain of Anglo misogynist culture—political movements are what have allowed our writing to surface from the secret places in our notebooks into the public sphere. In 1990, Chicanos, gay men, and women are not better off than we were in 1970. We have an ever-expanding list of physical and social diseases affecting us: AIDS, breast cancer, police brutality. Censorship is becoming increasingly institutionalized, not only through government programs, but through transnational corporate ownership of publishing houses, record companies, etc. Without a movement to foster and sustain our writing, we risk being swallowed up into the "Decade of the Hispanic" that never happened. The fact that a few of us have "made it" and are doing better than we imagined has not altered the nature of the beast. He remains blue-eyed and male and prefers profit over people.

Like most artists, we Chicano artists would like our work to be seen as "universal" in scope and meaning and reach as large an audience as possible. Ironically, the most "universal" work—writing capable of reaching the hearts of the greatest number of people—is the most culturally specific. The European-American writer understands this because it is his version of cultural specificity that is deemed "universal" by the literary establishment. In the same manner, universality in the *Chicana* writer requires the most Mexican and the most female images we are capable of producing. Our task is to write what no one is prepared to hear, for what has been said so far in barely a decade of consistent production is a mere bocadito. Chicana writers are still learning the art of transcription, but what we will be capable of producing in the decades to come, if we have the cultural/political movements to support us, could make a profound contribution to the social transformation of these Américas. The reto, however, is to remain as culturally specific and culturally complex as possible, even in the face of mainstream seduction to do otherwise.

Let's not fool ourselves, the European-American middle-class writer is the cultural mirror through which the literary and theatre establishment sees itself reflected, so it will continue to reproduce itself through new generations of writers. On occasion New York publishes our work, as it perceives a growing market for the material, allowing Chicanos access to national distribution on a scale that small independent presses could never accomplish. (Every writer longs for such distribution, particularly since it more effectively reaches communities of color.) But I fear that my generation and the generation of young writers that follows will look solely to the Northeast for recognition. I fear that we may become accustomed to this very distorted reflection, and that we will find ourselves writing more and more in translation through the filter of Anglo-American censors. Wherever Chicanos may live, in the richest and most inspired junctures of our writing, our writer-souls are turned away from Washington, the U.S. capital, and toward a México Antiguo. That is not to say that contemporary Chicano literature does not wrestle with current social concerns, but without the memory of our once-freedom, how do we imagine a future?

I still believe in a Chicano literature that is hungry for change, that has the courage to name the sources of our discontent both from within our raza and without, that challenges us to envision a world where poverty, crack, and pesticide poisoning are not endemic to people with dark skin or Spanish surnames. It is a literature that knows that god is neither white nor male nor reason to rape anyone. If such ideas are "naive," (as some critics would have us believe) then let us remain naive, naively and passionately committed to an art of "resistance," resistance to domination by Anglo-America, resistance to assimilation, resistance to economic and sexual exploitation. *An art that subscribes to integration into mainstream Amerika is not Chicano art.*

.....

All writing is confession. Confession masked and revealed in the voices and faces of our characters. All is hunger. The longing to be known fully and still loved. The admission of our own inherent vulnerability, our weakness, our tenderness of skin, fragility of heart, our overwhelming desire to be relieved of the burden of ourselves in the body of another, to be forgiven of our ultimate aloneness in the mystical body of a god or the common work of a revolution. These are human considerations that the best of writers presses her finger upon. The wound ruptures and... heals.

One of the deepest wounds Chicanos suffer is separation from our Southern relatives. Gloria Anzaldúa calls it a "1,950-mile-long open wound," dividing México from the United States, "dividing a *pueblo,* a culture." This "llaga" ruptures over and over again in our writing, Chicanos in search of a México that never wholly embraces us. "Mexico gags," poet Lorna Dee Cervantes writes, "on this bland pocha seed." This separation was never our choice. In 1990, we witnessed a fractured and disintegrating América, where the Northern half functions as the absentee landlord of the Southern half and the economic disparity between the First and Third Worlds drives a bitter wedge between a people.

I hold a vision requiring a radical transformation of consciousness in this country, that as the people-of-color population increases, we will not be just another brown faceless mass hungrily awaiting integration into white Amerika, but that we will emerge as a mass movement of people to redefine what an "American" is. Our entire concept of this nation's identity must change, possibly be obliterated. We must learn to see ourselves less as U.S. citizens and more as members of a larger world community composed of many nations of people and no longer give credence to the geopolitical borders that have divided us, Chicano from Mexicano, Filipino-American from Pacific Islander, African-American from Haitian. Call it racial memory. Call it shared economic discrimination. Chicanos call it "Raza,"—be it Quichua, Cubano, or Colombiano—an identity that dissolves borders. As a Chicana writer that's the context in which I want to create.

I am an American writer in the original sense of the word, an Américan *con acento.*

La Fuerza
Femenina

Credo

Frente al altar de mi madre
burning beads
de lágrimas cling
to the frozen face
of glass, flame quaking
in the wake
of the meeting
of mothers.

Tenemos el mismo problema,
the one says to the other
sin saber the meaning.

Each, their youngest daughter
a heretic
a non-believer.

But when you raised the burning
bush of cedar
our faces twin moons in the black night
I believed and dreamed
my body stripped naked
like the virgin daughter
splayed upon your altar.

Not that you, my priestess
would wrench from me
my heart sangrando
but to feel your hand heavy
on that raised hill
of flesh

my breast
rising

like a pyramid
from the sacred
walls of this templo

my body.

Blood Sisters

I remember a love once germinated outside the womb.
No blood ties that knot and strangle the heart,
but two soul sisters instantly joined
pressing wound against wound in tribal solemnity.

The first already broken open, beginning to scab.
The other, the braver—the young yielding lamb—
performing the ritual with any object
capable of cutting flesh.

she:
I dig at it, esta herida vieja
remind it to bleed
*this time with your name upon its lip*s

she:
obsidian, hermana
you, the dark mirror that splits my breast

Love has always been a sacrificial rite,
the surrender of one's heart to a merciless mother-god
who never forgave us our fleshy mortality
our sin of skin and bone, our desire
to meld them into miracles of something
else
not woman.

If

If in the long run
we weep together
hold each other
wipe the other's mouth
dry from the kiss pressed there
to seal the touch
of spirits separated
by something as necessary
as time

we will have done enough.

En busca de la fuerza femenina

I have just returned from the CARA exhibit and birthday dinner with Ricardo.[*] I had asked him to come with me, somehow knowing he was the spirit-brother to take, the one with whom to

[*]This essay was originally written for the Symposium on Current Debates in Chicano Culture on July 20, 1991. The symposium was organized by the Mexican Museum in conjunction with the exhibition, "Chicano Art: Resistance and Affirmation 1965–1985" at the San Francisco Museum of Modern Art. Ricardo Bracho is a poet and activist who lives in the Bay Area.

witness our past in order to reconstruct a future. Ricardo: 22 years old today, Chicano, and gay.

And we felt such pride upon entering the gallery from the sight of the first image: "¡VIVA LA RAZA!" it proclaimed. The "VIVA" spread across the canvas in bold black splashes, the enflamed red Chicano eagle rising. "Orgullo" was the word that kept shaping in my chest, expanding in my throat until it spilled out from my lips. "I'm so damn proud," I say. To witness a living art, an art molded out of our brown and multifarious lives.

The exhibit opened to a world of color, like the México I had just returned from days before. There was no shyness, no inhibition, no Anglo beige. Ponemos el color dondequiera—like the colors that paint the courtyard walls of San Cristóbal, like the richest colors at the hour of a Oaxacan sunset; like the light landing onto the bougainvillaea, onto the curve of Tarascan nose and cheekbone, onto the huipil of Zapotec women. I experienced there in the artwork the same México, its Indian territory emblazoned upon graffitied walls, pressed into the creased edges of José Montoya's "drapes," gestating in Yreina Cervantes' exposed wombs of Native mothers. And the Earth quakes, remembering...

I didn't know I was lonely, I had forgotten. I had forgotten I was without a country. I had forgotten I had lost a language. For a moment...until I saw the word "CHICANO" in bold orange and red letters on Van Ness Avenue in downtown San Panchito, Aztlán* and

---

*"San Panchito" is Chicano slang for San Francisco. I describe "Aztlán" as the Chicano homeland further in the essay, "Queer Aztlán: The Re-formation of Chicano Tribe," which appears later in this collection.

my territory was righteously reclaimed by my sister and brother artists.

And yet, something was missing... Artist Rupert García noted the same when he said that the show did not immediately inspire him to pick up the paintbrush. It did, however, inspire *me* to pick up the *pen*. I was going to write, "the pain, to pick up the pain." That, for me, was what was missing. An honest portrait of our pain.

After resistance and affirmation, where do we go? Possibly to a place of deeper inquiry into ourselves as a people. Possibly, as we move into the next century, we must turn our eyes away from racist Amerika and take stock of the damages done us. Possibly the greatest risks yet to be taken are *entre nosotros,* where we write, paint, dance, and draw the wound for one another in order to build a stronger pueblo. The women artists seemed disposed to do this, their work often mediating that delicate area between cultural affirmation and criticism.

What was missing in this exhibit was the rage and revenge of women, the recognition that the violence of racism and misogyny has distorted our view of ourselves.[*] What was missing was a portrait of sexuality for men and women independent of motherhood and machismo: images of the male body as violador *and* vulnerable, and of the female body as the site of woman-centered desire. There was no visible gay and lesbian response to our chicanidad that would challenge institutionalized and mindless heterosexual coupling; no

---

[*]One notable exception was Celia Rodríguez' "La Llorona." The watercolor figure appears with a bundle, which the artist calls "her constant companion, symbolizing loss and psychic suffering." La Llorona's burden is identified as specifically female and mestiza.

break-down and shake-up of La Familia y La Iglesia; no portrait of our isolation, of machismo as monstruo, of la Indígena erased and muted in the body of la Chicana.

.....

Sometimes when I write, I feel I am drawing from the most silent place in myself—a place without image, word, shape, sound—to create a portrait of la Mechicana before the "Fall," before shame, before betrayal, before Eve, Malinche, and Guadalupe; before the occupation of Aztlán, la llegada de los españoles, the Aztecs' War of Flowers. I don't know what this woman looks like exactly, but I know she is more than the bent back in the fields, more than the assembly-line fingers and the rigid body beneath him in bed, more than the veiled face above the rosary beads. She is more than the sum of all these fragmented parts.

As Chicana artists, our efforts to imag(in)e what has never been portrayed is a deeply spiritual quest. Like every male artist— Chicano, Anglo, or otherwise—we women artists also look for god in our work. We too ultimately seek the divine in the beauty we create. Sometimes that beauty is merely a portrait of mutilation in color or language. This is something Frida Kahlo understood. For the road to the female god is wrought with hatred, humiliation, and heartbreak.

How did we become so broken?

.....

*El mito azteca**

Según la leyenda, Coatlicue, "Madre de los Dioses," is sweeping on top of the mountain, Coatepec, when she discovers two beautiful feathers. Thinking that later she will place them on her altar, she stuffs them into her apron and continues sweeping. But without noticing, the feathers begin to gestate there next to her womb and Coatlicue, already advanced in age, soon discovers that she is pregnant.

When her daughter, Coyolxauhqui, learns that her mother is about to give birth to Huitzilopotchli, God of War, she is incensed. And, along with her siblings, the Four Hundred Stars, she conspires to kill Coatlicue rather than submit to a world where War would become God.

Huitzilopotchli is warned of this by a hummingbird and vows to defend his mother. At the moment of birth, he murders Coyolxauhqui, cutting off her head and completely dismembering her body.

Breast splits from chest splits from hip splits from thigh from knee from arm and foot. Coyolxauhqui is banished to the darkness and becomes the moon, la diosa de la luna.

In my own art, I am writing that wound. That moment when brother is born and sister mutilated by his envy. He possesses the

*Thanks to Mexican performance artist Guadalupe García, who first introduced this myth to me.

mother, holds her captive, because she cannot refuse any of her children, even her enemy son. Here, mother and daughter are pitted against each other and daughter must kill male-defined motherhood in order to save the culture from misogyny, war, and greed. But el hijo comes to the defense of patriarchal motherhood, kills la mujer rebelde, and female power is eclipsed by the rising light of the Sun/Son. This machista myth is enacted every day of our lives, every day that the sun (Huitzilopotchli) rises up from the horizon and the moon (Coyolxauhqui) is obliterated by his light.

Huitzilopotchli is not my god. And although I revere his mother, Coatlicue, Diosa de La Muerte y La Vida, I do not pray to her. I pray to the daughter, La Hija Rebelde. She who has been banished, the mutilated sister who transforms herself into the moon. She is la fuerza femenina, our attempt to pick up the fragments of our dismembered womanhood and reconstitute ourselves. She is the Chicana writer's words, the Chicana painter's canvas, the Chicana dancer's step. She is motherhood reclaimed and sisterhood honored. She is the female god we seek in our work, la Mechicana before the "fall."

And Huitzilopotchli raises his sword from the mouth of his mother's womb and cuts off his sister's head, her bleeding down the belly of the serpent-mountain. Coyolxauhqui, moon-faced goddess, enters the darkness, y la Raza, la época de guerra.

Pero de vez en cuando la luna gets her revenge.

. . . . .

Just a week ago, I returned from a two-month stay in México, the last day of which found me on top of a pyramid in Tepotzlán, an hour outside of Mexico City. At 1:26 pm the sky fell to complete darkness as the moon eclipsed the sun. "Tonatiuh cualo, " el sol fue comido por la fuerza femenina. And el Conchero* who led the ceremonia in full Aztec regalia de pluma y piel believed it an ominous sign, this momentary and sudden loss of light, this deep silent feminine darkness. The quieting of the pájaros, the retreat of the ground animals into their caves of night. And he prayed to the gods to return the light. And I prayed with him, brother that he is, brother who never recognizes his sister in prayer, brother who fears her power, as mother and daughter and wife and lover, as he fears the darkening of the light.

But we women were not afraid, accustomed as we are to the darkness. In public, we mouthed the shapes of his words that mourned the loss of light, and in secret we sang praise to She Who Went Unacknowledged, She Who Remains in Shadow, She Who Has the Power to Put Out the Sun's Light. Coyolxauhqui, the moon, reduced in newspapers to the image of a seductress, flirtatious coquette, merging in coitus with the sun. Later, we women, lesbianas from all parts of América Latina, would offer sacrifice, burn copal, call out her name. We, her sisters, would pay tribute to la luna, keep the flame burning, keep destruction at bay.

In those six minutes of darkness, something was born. In the darkness of that womb of silence, that female quietude, a life stirred.

---

*A "conchero" is a ceremonial leader who sounds the conch shell and leads the people in their prayers and offerings.

I understood for the first time the depth and wonder of the feminine, although I confess I have been awed by it before, as my own female face gazes upon its glory and I press my lips to that apex in the women I love.

Like the others, I welcomed the light upon its return. El Canto del Gallo. Probably that was the most amazing of all, el segundo amanecer. The female passed on y dió luz a un sol nuevo. As the light took the shape of the sky again, el Conchero stood on top of the pyramid mountain and announced the end of El Quinto Sol, the end of a 500-year historia sangrienta that saw to the near destruction of the Indigenous peoples of Las Américas. And from the ashes of destruction, a new era is born: El Sexto Sol: La Epoca de La Conciencia Humana.

·····

The day after the eclipse, I called my mother from San Francisco to tell her I had arrived home safely. And without planning to, when describing the eclipse I told her, "Ahora conozco a Dios, Mamá." And I knew she understood my reverence in the face of a power utterly beyond my control. She is a deeply religious woman, who calls her faith "catholic." I use another name or no name, but she understood that humility, that surrender, before a sudden glimpsed god. Little did she know god was a woman.

I am not the church-goer that my mother is, but the same faithfulness drives me to write: the search for Coyolxauhqui amid all the disfigured female characters and the broken men that surround them in my plays and poems. I search for a whole woman I can shape with my own Chicana tongue and hand. A free citizen of Aztlán and the world.

La Ofrenda

Strange as it may seem, there is no other way to be sure. Completely sure. Well, you can never be completely sure but you can try and hold fast to some things. Smell is very important. Your eyes can fool you. You can see things that aren't there. But not smell. Smell remembers and tells the future. No lying about that.

Smell can make your heart crack open no matter how many locks you have wrapped 'round it. You can't see smell coming so it takes you off guard, unaware. Like love. That's why it can be your best friend or worst enemy depending on the state of your heart at the time.

Smell is home or loneliness.
Confidence or betrayal.
Smell remembers.

.....

Tiny never went with women because she decided to. She'd always just say, "I follow my nose." And she did and it got her ass nearly burned plenty of times, too, when the scent happened to take her to the wrong side of town or into the bed of the wife of someone she'd wish it hadn't in the morning.

She hated to fight. That was the other problem. She never stuck around for a fight. "The only blood I like," she'd say, "is what my hand digs out of a satisfied woman." We'd all tell Tiny to shut her arrogant mouth up and get her another drink.

Christina Morena, who stood in front of me in the First Holy Communion line. Then, by confirmation, Tiny'd left most of us girls in the dust. Shot up and out like nobody's business. So Christina, who everyone called Tina, turned to Tiny overnight and that's the name she took with her into "the life." Given her size, it was a better name to use than Christina and certainly better than mine, Dolores. Dottie, they used to call me years later in some circles, but it never stuck, cuz I was the farthest thing from a freckled-faced bony-kneed gabacha. Still, for a while I tried it. Now I'm back to who I was before. Just Lolita. Stripped down. Not so different from those Holy Communion days, really.

When we were kids, teenagers, we came *this* close to making it with each other. *This* close. I don't know what would've happened if we had, but I couldn't even've dreamed of doing it then. Yeah, I loved Tiny probably more than I loved any human being on the face of the earth. I mean I loved her like the way you love familia like they could do anything—steal, cheat, lie, murder and you'd still love them because they're your blood. Sangre. Tiny was my blood. My blood sister. Maybe that's why we didn't do it back then. It'd be like doing it with your mother. No, your sister. Tiny was my sister like no sister I've ever had and she wanted me and I left her because she'd rather pretend she didn't and I was too stupid to smell out the situation for what it really was. I kept watching what was coming outta her damn mouth and there wasn't nothing there to hear. No words of love, commitment, tenderness. You know, luna de miel stuff. There was just her damn solid square body like a tank in the middle of my face with tears running down her cheeks and her knees squeezed together like they were nailed shut on that toilet, her pants like a rubber band wrapped down around her ankles and I ran from her as fast as my cola could take me.

"Fuck fuck chinga'o, man, fuck!"
"Tina…" I can barely hear myself.
"Tiny. The name's Tiny."
"What're you doin' in there?"
"I'm crying, you faggot. That's what you want, isn't it? To see the big bad bitch cry? Well, go get your rocks off somewhere else."
"I don't have rocks."
"In your head!"

But I never loved anyone like I loved Tiny. No body. Not one of those lean white or fine black ladies that spread their legs for me and my smooth-talking. There was blood on my hands and not from reaching into those women but from Tiny's hide. From my barrio's hide. From Cha Cha's Place where you only saw my ass when the sophisticated college girls had fucked with my mind one too many times. That's something Tiny would have said. We weren't meant to be lovers, only sisters. But being a sister ain't no part-time occupation.

"Lolita Lebrón." That's what they used to call me at Cha Cha's. Of course, they didn't even know who Lolita was until I came in with the story of her with the guys and the guns taking on the whole pinche U.S. Congress. They'd say, "Hey, Lolita, how goes the revolution?" And then they'd all start busting up and I'd take it cuz I knew they loved me, even respected what I was doing. Or maybe it was only Tiny who respected me and all the others had to treat me right cuz of her. Tiny used to say her contribution to La Causa was to keep the girlfriends of the Machos happy while they were out being too revolutionary to screw.

But it was me she wanted. And I needed my original home girl more than I needed any other human being alive to this day. Growing up is learning to go without. Tiny and me…we grew up too fast.

.....

"Do you think Angie could want me?"

So there we are, fifteen years later, me sitting on the edge of her bed, playing with the little raised parts of the chenille bedspread while my sister there is taking off all her damn clothes, tossing them onto the bed, until she's standing bare ass naked in front of me.

"Look at me."
I can't look up.
"Lola."
I'm still playing with the balls on the bedspread.
"Look at me. C'mon I gotta know."
"Tiny give me a break, man, this is too cold. It's fuckin' scientific, no one looks at people this way."
"You do."

She was right. So, I check her out. There I am staring at her with my two good eyes, the blue one and the brown one and I knew she wanted my 100 percent true and honest opinion that she could count on me for that since we were little, so I sat there looking at her for a long time.

"C'mon, man, does it hafta take so long? Jus' answer me."

The blue and the brown eye were working at this one, working hard. I try to isolate each eye, see if I come up with different conclusions depending on which eye and which color I'm working with. Figure one is the European view, the other the Indian.

Tiny goes for her pants, "Fuck you."

And then I smell her, just as she reaches over me. Her breast brushing my shoulder, a warm bruised stone…something softening. I inhale. Grab her arm. "No, wait. Let me look at you."

She pulls back against the dresser, holds the pants against her belly, then lets them drop. She's absolutely beautiful. Not magazine beautiful, but thirty-three years old and Mexican beautiful. The dresser with the mirror is behind her. I know that dresser. For years now. It didn't change, but Tiny...she did. The dresser is blonde. "Blonde furniture," very popular among Mexicanos in the fifties. We are the children of the fifties. But the fifties have gone and went and in the meantime my Christina Morena went and changed herself into a woman. And in front of this blonde dresser is brown Christina. Christina Morena desnuda sin a stitch on her body and she looks like her mother and my mother with legs like tree trunks and a panza that rolls round into her ombligo como pura miel. And breasts...breasts I want to give back to her, compartir con ella que nos llenan a las dos.

"Well...?" she asks.

And it had never occurred to me that we had grown up. The hair below the hill of her belly is the same color as her head. A deep black. Denso. Oculto como un nido escondido. Un hogar distante, aguardándome.

It didn't stop there. She needed me to touch her, that's all. Is that so much to ask of a person? Angie and her wouldn't last long. Tiny didn't let her touch her. She never let any of 'em touch her.

"Never?"
"Never."
"I don't get it. What do you do then?"

"I do it *to* them."

"But I mean do you...y'know."

"Get off? Yeah. Sure."

"How?"

"Rubbing. Thinking."

"Thinking. Thinking about what?"

"Her. How she's feeling."

"You ever think about yourself?"

"No one's home."

"What?"

"I don't gotta picture, you know what I mean? There's nobody to be. No me to be...not in the bed, anyway."

So, I put my hands inside her. I did. I put them all the way inside her and like a fuckin' shaman I am working magic on her, giving her someone to be.

"Fuck fuck chinga'o man, fuck."

"Shut up," I say.

"What?"

"Don't say shit."

"But..."

"Shhhhh." I press my fingers against her lips. "Don't say nothing, Tiny." Open your mouth and tell me something else...

She smells like copal between the legs. Tiny, Tina who stood in front of me in the First Holy Communion line, smells like fucking copal

sweet earth sap

oozing outta every pore

that dark bark tree
flesh kissed
I couldn't kiss her, only between the legs
where the mouth there never cussed
where the lips there never curled
into snarls, smoked cigarettes, spit
phlegm into passing pale stubbled faces
mouthing dagger
dyke
jota
mal
flor
I kissed her where she had never spoken
where she had never sang
where...

and then we are supposed to forget. Forget the women we discover there between the sheets, between the thighs, lies, cries. But some things you don't forget

smell.

I close my eyes and I am rubbing and thinking rubbing and thinking rubbing and remembering what this feels like, to find my body, una vega anhelosa, endless llano de deseo

¿Dónde 'stá ella que me regaló mi cuerpo como una ofrenda a mí misma?

Ella

Lejana.

Una vez, mía.

I open my eyes…Desaparecida.

I would've married Tiny myself if she would've let me. I would've. I swear to it. But I was relieved when she put on her pants and told me to get out. I was relieved because I wouldn't have to work for the rest of my life loving someone. Tiny.

But I *was* willing to stay. This time I wasn't going nowhere. I mean, where was there to go, really? The girl was family and I knew her. I knew her and *still* loved her, so where was there to go? You spend your whole life looking for something that's just a simple matter of saying, "Okay, so I throw my lot in with this one." This one woman y ya!

.....

Tiny knew she wouldn't last that long.

She was already telling me in her thirties how tired she was, fighting. And then I read it, right there in the *L.A. Times.* All these women, lesbians who never had babies, getting cancer. They never mention Tiny's name, but Tiny was there, among the childless women, among the dead.

I thought, what's *this* shit? Women don't use their breasts like biology mandates, and their breasts betray them? Is this the lesbian castigo? AIDS for our brothers, cancer for us? Hate thinking like this, hate thinking it's all a conspiracy to make us join the fucking human race.

I burn copal.
Her name rising up with the smoke,
dissolving into the ash morning sky.
Her flesh softening like sap
over rock, returning liquid
to the earth. Her scent inciting...

memory.

I inscribe my name, too.
Tattooed ink in the odorless flesh of this page.

I, who have only given my breast
to the hungry and grown,
the female and starved
the women.

I, who have only given my breast to the women.

The Breakdown of the Bicultural Mind

Mestizos, children of violence,
neither slaves nor masters.
— Chilam Balam

Sueño

I *have been at an amusement park. On my way home, I stop to buy something at a small tiendita. There is a thin young girl working the register. It is a family store. This is her home. Other family members are nearby. She tells me the purchase costs 300, but I am confused. Does she mean 300 dollars, cents, pesos? She keeps changing the amount and I keep apologizing, thinking at one point she means pesos, then realizing 300 pesos is nothing, then realizing I am not in México, but possibly Puerto Rico where the currency is dollars. Then I see that the girl is merely trying to cheat me.*

My response is to take out paints and give the family a chance to use them. The father sits at the opposite end of the table from the son. They begin to paint. All is the color red. As the father works, his paints spill like blood all over the table. I realize now how hard it has been for the family. The man is very thin, frail, sickly. As he bleeds into the page, the red runs. The boy manages to keep most of his drawing unstained by the father's. I see the son protecting his painting, shielding it from the father's with his forearm. His picture is very neat. There is the image of a flower. When the drawing is done, the boy has disappeared and the father retreats to the next room, but the old man is still visible and within earshot.

Now the older sisters are at the table. The young girl joins them. I see her painting. It is pages and pages of blood red writing. She did not draw, but wrote her story in images of words. I spy the word "testicles," and I know on some level the story has to do with the father's pain. After finishing her painting, the girl is very shaken. I take her under my arm, bring her to the couch. I hold her and tell her, "We're going to read this out loud, so that you can get it off of you, so that you can be free of his pain." (I am conscious of speaking softly so that the father does not hear, but he is aware of our presence.) The older sisters say they must go, that they can't bear to hear the story. I understand. And as I press the girl next to me, I begin to read aloud...

Peloncito

there is a man in my life
pale-man born infant
pliable flesh his body remains
a remote possibility

in secret it may know many things
glossy newsprint female thighs
spread eagle wings
in his flying imagination

soft shoe
he did the soft shoe
in the arch that separated the living
from dining room
miller trombone still turns his heel
and daughter barefoot and never pregnant
around and around and around

soft-tip
penis head he had
a soft-tipped penis that peeked out
accidentally one kitchen cold morning
between zipper stuck and boxer shorts
fresh pressed heat lining those tender white-meat loins

wife at the ironing board:

"what are you doing, jim, what are you doing?"
he nervously stuffs the little bird back

it looked like *Peloncito*
the bald-headed little name
of my abuelita's pajarito

Peloncito
a word of endearment
never told to the child/
father/ yellow bird-man/
boy

If a Stranger Could Be Called Family

There *are* men in my life.

Inconsequential, I reason.
Their histories silenced between the sheets
of frozen intercourse who lie in the morning
about who came to their bed last night
what dark stranger's drink did he taste upon his lips
he won't tell

unlike the wife, he has no stories
only memories glossed and nostalgic:
the loving mother
the absent, but distinguished father.

.....

Now once there was the glimpsed image
of a trolley car blur of san francisco technicolor
12-year-old boy sitting with little sister
decently dressed depression years,
not a word outta him from Judah to Market.

"He'd never speak to me," the sister complained.
It was *her* story, she the protagonist in search
of a brother a lover a man

his boy shoulders
folded into the broad leaves
of a book.

.....

Now an old man whose middle age I've forgotten
he tells a few stories once in a blue
although he's never learned the Mexican art,
grandchildren fidgeting restlessly in straight-backed chairs.
His older, more generous offspring patiently wait out
the long lapses in memory the punch line
slipping precipitously
from his pressed lips.

The old man, he tries.
We patronize
apologize.

.....

But once there was a story
not a story exactly, but a picture
he remembered the naked legs of a man in a bathrobe
and a word he had awoken to in the morning,
"uncle"

and there would be many many "uncles" to follow
long lines of them
faceless

behind the seamless door
of his mother's bedroom.

If a stranger could be called "uncle," what was family worth?

.....

Today on visit to his native
San Francisco
we roll by Geary Theatre
he remembers it 1930s
mother in her silk kimono
exotic in the vestiges of her vaudeville days
her son waxes nostalgic like an old lover
a young suitor.

"She was nothing special," the back-seat wife whispers
"I don't think they ever put her on the stage even..."
she was nothing nothing
what little legacy we orphans
my father and I have
shattered.

I point to the small theatre across the street.
It is nothing nothing special,
but there I will tell *their* stories
lies, nostalgia, and the whole ball of wax
because we all got a story
we all each one got a story
to tell.

I Was Not Supposed to Remember

the smell of geraniums
what perfume penetrates nostrils not grown
from a bottle 'n' mother's wrists 'n' just a dab
behind each ear I was not supposed to remember her ears
like mine, the earlobe without lobe really
the mole that marked her
mine.

I was not supposed to remember being she
the daughter of some other Indian some body some where
an orphaned child somewhere somebody's
cast-off half-breed I wasn't
supposed to remember the original rape.

I wasn't supposed to remember
my whitedaddy and baby's cry
my white father's own orphanhood.
I was never to see my self reflected
in the cold steel frightened fluttering
I was not intended
to marry that man.

.....

I am a woman, childless
and I teach my stories to other

childless women and somehow
the generations will propagate and prosper
and remember pre-memory

remember rose gardens thorn-pricked thumbs digging
into well-watered southern california soil kissing
the edge of steaming black-top

what *is* there left to remember
of those days
what *is* there left

to dirt *How is it I remember*
dirt when I grew up on asphalt?
How is it dirt means so much to me?
What is there to remember in a tree?

a tree
thoroughly tree

I, thoroughly hybrid
mongrel/mexicanyaqui/oakie girl.
"Yaquioakie" holds all the world
I knew as it shaped my abuela's lips
calling in my breed-brother
thorough-bred primo,
sandy wool y pelos de indio
bent over bowls of albóndigas soup.

.....

Mongrel is the name
that holds all the animal I am.
My legs split open straddling
the examination table she tells me
your fibroid ain't no watermelon
just the size of a small navel orange
and I consider this sphere of influence
steadily growing behind my own navel
little satellites of smaller fibroids
floating inside its citric orbit.

I imagine the color/the taste of fruit/the bitterness
of peel and pleasure   there *is* pleasured familiarity
as she moves her dark safe-sexed-gloved hand
up inside me   a lesbian gesture
I, a lesbian monster
she recommends hormones
have you always been this hairy
yes, I say, I remember since I became a woman
with hair lots of it does that make a woman
or a lesbian
or an animal?

which brings me back to mongrel
and the hybrid sheep-goat I saw
in a magazine once
with pitiful pleading eyes
trying to bust out
of her genetically altered face

and I saw my face in there
no matter how much I am loved
no matter how much woman
I am no matter how many women
hold and suck me
I am mirrored in those pitiful
lonesome
product of mutation
eyes.

Whose Savior?

I hate white people.
White blood.

Hate the rape carved into this one's
delicate nose, that one's shock
of blonde wooly hair/hazel
eyes, the pink spots
that blotch my cheeks and hands
in the bitterest of winters—
secret signs surfacing
making few people safe
brothers
familia.

The white people I am are not rich.
Are freckled
pale
overweight
polyestered and without
class
or good genes.
They do not know how to dress.

They are not romantic.
They are not the rugged-boned women I've seen
in picket-line photos of the thirties
arm 'n arm with negro church women

chicano miners' wives.
Sturdy bent backs
flowered dresses flapping
in brisk breezes.

The white people I am have sucked dry
the bones of the colored
worn their own resistance down
by a quiet weak-kneedness
made to resemble patience.

What *are* they waiting for,
these white folks?

Whose savior's gonna come get us?

Half-breed

the difference between you and me
is as I bent over strangers' toilet bowls,
the face that glared back at me
in those sedentary waters
was not my own,
but my mother's
brown bead floating in a soon pool
of crystalline whiteness

she taught me how to clean
to get down on my hands and knees
and scrub, not beg

she taught me how to clean,
not live in this body

my reflection has always been
once removed.

It's Not New York

It is a chinese diner that serves grey
american hamburgers, garlic-spread bread, pale
chicken rice soup, watered-down
ice tea. We have it all.
The homegirl and I eat
and sit cross-eyed from each other
vinyl-checkered tablecloth beneath our elbows, we wave
forks she, a spoon and we talk like this could be any city
where my bed waits for me could be 1,000 miles away.
It doesn't matter.

Pouring rain outside the restaurant plate glass.
I have to prove this to her, make her
turn and look the other way, see
the rain through the glare of taxi-cab headlights.
It could be new york. It's not.
And she sees and agrees.
Rivers of gutter rain.

This is joy.
It has the name and look of her,
her black eyes, my childhood eyes staring back at me
and nothing in our mutual L.A. sub-urban pasts prepared us
for this moment of neon-rippled reflection
off store-front windows, brake lights swimming in pools
of black liquid, umbrellas competing

for headroom on sidewalks.

Theatre surrounds us.
We talk and talk and all
is complete. The circle of her moonface
holding vigil to mine. If we touch hands,
it is not a plea but an electric acknowledgment:

I was there, too.
The long hot drives home from Fresno to L.A.,
the half-breed cousins mexicans mothers
thinking spanish talking spanglish teaching english
to their children. The two of us
bony-elbowed grace in the back of the station wagon
57 buick, the fleshy backs of our arms
sticking like bandaids
we pull away from each other,
giggle and slide back in again.
I see you, homegirl, behind the gas station,
bruised kneecap against my chest, you got me down
your hands, brown cuffs of flesh around my wrists, I twist
and squirm, I twist and squirm, the crab grass itching my back.

Tougher always tougher than me
your face softens and when you bend to kiss me,
I don't turn away.

Indian Summer

Barely midday and the sun has already moved behind the cedar tree. Watering time so tomato leaves won't burn from direct light, so the soil don't soak up the liquid life like so much sponge.

I watch her through my window. She got a way with that hose and hoe. She got a way of turning country on me. She a big girl. No nonsense. Wielding that liquid tongue like she the fertility goddess herself.

"You act like you own it," I shout out to her.
"What?"
"That garden."

"No, baby. I'm only a squatter. Squatter's rights is all it is, but I intend to assert them." I love that kind of talk. It'd be hard to be without that talk.

She's got the hose now wrapped 'round her naked shin, twisted up between her legs, mud splattered around her ankles and those tired-ass sandals. I'll be wiping up their tracks again once she comes back inside.

"You can't stay here." That's the first thing out of her mouth as she puts one muddy paw inside the front door. I like living like this, always on the edge of her throwing me out.

"Why now?"

"Cuz I'm getting too attached, that's why. The garden's growing. The tomatoes are on the verge of ripening and you're gonna leave me anyway, so get out now." She's not even mad, even grinning a little bit. Mud smudges just above the left side of her lip. She's a wild whitegirl.

"It's only for a month," I bargain.

"You won't even be here to see the tomatoes turn." She's pouting.

"I regret that," I say.

"Regret. Right." She's working herself into a serious pout now. I grab her by the hip, slide my hand into the back pocket of her jeans shorts.

"Sit down." I pull her onto my lap. She puts her face inside the hollow of my neck. This is the dance we do.

"Let's bury it," she says.

"What?"

"This 'relationship' routine. All you desperate wounded butches who can't make up your damn minds. I'm tired of it." She's got a hold of her ankle now and is wiping the mud from it with a saliva-tipped finger.

I want that finger in my mouth, that mud. I start to my feet, she slides off of me.

"You can't stay here," she says. "I warn you."

The Grass, Not Greener

In dreams
that take me away from you
we are a different two
women, mestizas traveling in the land
that is at once ours and stolen
and we live daily in the moment of that
highway robbery
on each side, a desert claimed
and disturbed.

I confess my dreams look like this,
what is *not* outside our mutual morning
window of shipyard, loading dock, warehouses
of corrugated aluminum roof.

I cannot stay here forever.
But will you take me with you?
you ask.

My life and yours is a prayer.
I live it daily as the last one
said before parting into another world
whose terrain we can only guess.
I imagine the grass, not greener
only the earth, more yielding to a native daughter's
step and dance.

Today I think of leaving you, I won't.
Because today is a grey August San Francisco morning
that tricks us into winter feelings. And one does not leave
in winter when flesh assumes the texture of covers
dense and delicate where the curve
and simple weight of one breast folded into the arc
of rib cage is sufficient to keep me
hours longer still not moving
into this deceptive day.

If I could love you as a mother
I would be the best of lovers.
Preparing your morning tea, I dream
of the woman you want to be.
I see her take shape in the thickening
of your hands, peasant hands.
We grow middle-aged together.

But in eyes the color of sea
you sail away.
I stand on the shore's edge,
the desert plains behind me.

I wave good-bye eternally.

The Breakdown of the Bicultural Mind

Like many other prophetic leaders of nativistic movements, be they Moses...or Malcolm X, the intensity of the vision seems to be fired by the internal conflict coming from a culturally mixed parentage.
— William Irwin Thompson,
Blue Jade from the Morning Star

I read all I can for a clue. Looking to Moses and Malcolm to come up with some thread of connection, some sense of how my mixed-blood identity has driven me to politics, protest, and poetry, of why I awaken at three o'clock in the morning, a heaviness over my heart. *Who is sitting on my chest?*

I read of Quetzalcóatl—the story of the man, not the god, destined to relive, as Thompson writes, "the primal act of rape which brought his soul into the world." He compulsively re-enacts that history through sexual indulgences, subsequent penance, and submersion into the fire of transformation. And like the phoenix rising, Quetzalcóatl is reborn into the morning star.

I read and I remember. At nineteen, I first heard the story of the "mulatto," as my friend called him. A musician she knew who was born a black smudge into an otherwise lily-white family. No one ever spoke about it. He was never told he was Black, but figured it out in a life in and out of prison, drugs, and jazz clubs. And then one night, alone in his apartment and thrashing so bad inside, he went, without thinking, into the bathroom and filled the tub with scalding hot water. At the moment he submerged his body, long legs and back, then face into the water, he remembered. He remembered being no bigger than the length of his mother's arm as she dropped him suffocating into the liquid flame. So the story goes, the next day the man sold all that he owned, including his precious saxophone, but kept his car to live and sleep in, never moving it. One morning they found him in it, gassed to death. *Sometimes one lifetime is not enough to repair the damage. That is what we fear, isn't it?*

The story stuck. Twenty years later and I'm still thinking about it. This mixed-blood scenario that ends in suicide, that ends in rebirth. What fiery pit awaits us, we new breed of 21st-century mestizo? Into what shapes shall we be transformed?

I re-read my own writings of a decade ago and see the same struggles. Then I was no less the mixed-blood Mexican, la mestiza's mestiza. The difference now is that I understand that my writer's journey is not strictly wedded to my individual story—the marriage of my U.S.-born Mexican mother of Sonora roots to my San Francisco-born French and British-Canadian father. That story alone does not explain my dreams, my nightmares, my insistent cultural nationalism. There is something older, something I remember and live out again and again in the women I love, the family I make, the poems and characters I create. Thompson goes on to write, "we are more than we know"; and there is consolation in this, that there may be a more powerful impetus than my mere forty-year-old biography to explain this unyielding need to re-live the rape, understand the rape, the loss...the truth.

We are no Moses, no Malcolm, no Queztalcóatl, but we are all our own gods. And our liberation won't happen by some man leading the way and parting the Red Sea for us. We are the Red Sea, we women.

.....

We Invent Ourselves

10 noviembre 1992

Lifting off home turf I don't really feel I am leaving home until I spy the moon, a San Francisco dawn's full moon, descending into the skyline. She speaks to me of longevity, a sisterguide in an otherwise lonesome horizon. But I recognize that horizon, know the geography of peninsula and bay and eastside hills, northside bridge (not gold, but orange) buried beneath fog caps. I know dotted islands of empty prison cells, processing camps, cruel welcomings, and land grabs.

My Spanish surname is chiseled into a tombstone on the breastbone of mission tiles and Indian dirt. There are whole city blocks with his name attached to them and we—whoever we I am with—invariably fantasize about coming in the middle of the night, stealing the signs and leaving the streets nameless and unoccupied. It is a lesbian dream, like the moon, grander than city planners' visions, than blueprints, than conquistador maps.

But what I really wanted to write about was that rising sun spilling out of the Oakland Hills, that moon resting on a cushion of coastal fog. You are not asleep yet, but will be soon, driving the little blue Toyota, gas tank near empty, back to our sleeping home.

.....

I have loved all kinds of women in all kinds of towns. Last night an old writer friend, a Southern woman, tells me over a meal of fried okra and chicken and polenta, *polenta's no more than grits, just a fancy name for grits*. But this is San Francisco (what-used-to-be-Black) upper Filmore, so polenta it is. I tell her, spooning the last of that upscale yellow mush into my mouth, *we've known a lot of women. Why is it so hard to write of what we know about women?* And much of what I know, I admit, is about race.

In love, color blurs but never wholly disappears. I have had only one great fear as a lesbian lover—that my eye would turn on my beloved, that I would see her through the stranger's eye, that what I fear in my own desire, its naked hunger, I would recoil from in her open-faced body.

And my eyes have *turned over and over again.*

I have never had a race-less relationship. Somehow I have always attributed this to being mixed-blood, but I wonder if anyone has. Maybe white people are the only ones in this country to enjoy the luxury of being "colorblind" with one another, white people in all the glory of their centrality. Not I. As deeply as I have feared the power of my infinite female darkness, feared my Mexican mutedness, feared my bottomless rage in my brown-skinned lovers, I have feared the mirror of my passivity, my orphanhood, my arrogance and ignorance in the white women I have loved. It is not a pretty picture. I have at times seen Black women as cold as any white woman in their "gringa" chauvinism, and I have seen Latinas as spineless as any man in their disloyalty to women. I have been both agringada and spineless and this is not a confession, but an unholy testament to my unwavering faith in lesbians to name from the bed those battles being waged on the street.

.....

We light-skinned breeds are like chameleons, those lagartijas with the capacity to change the color of their skins. We change not for lack of conviction, but lack of definitive shade and shape. My lovers have always been the environment that defined my color. With a Black lover in apartheid Boston I was seen as a whitegirl. When we moved to Brooklyn, we were both Ricans. In Harlem, I became "Spanish." In México, we were both Cubans. With my brown girlfriends we be brown girls sitting on brownstones. We be family. Among Indians in the States, I'm a half-breed who looks like every other breed, colored mixed with cowboy. Among Indians in México, I am güera, ladina, extranjera, and not to be trusted. Among Chicanas, I am everybody's cousin Carmen. Whitegirls change my shade to a paler version. People think I'm Italian, Jewish. In bed, I sizzle brown indifference, brown in difference. On downtown streets, I disappear grey into the color of sidewalk. No body notices me. For that reason, I got to be choosy 'bout who I hang with. Everybody so contagious, I pick up their gesture, their joke, their jive. We invent ourselves. A mixed-blood Hawaiian friend tells me, "I create whole biographies of the black childhood I never had. Give me enough time with you, I'll invent a Mexican one, too."

"The dark woman looking in through the glass is as frightened as I am. She is weeping. I will not let her in."

I remember Pacific Ocean Park in the fifties. She was a girl my age, my size. We stood in line for the "Wild Car" ride. I remember her darkness, her difference, her nappy hair corralled into three perfectly plaited pigtails. I didn't understand the third one. Why was it there? My mother always twisted my busterbrown straightness into two limp fountains spilling out from behind each ear, temples stretched to breaking point. So tight a hairdo, it could last for weeks. I didn't know about little black girls' hair and how their mothers sat them between their knees, greasing and separating and combing each section into that exact symmetry. So tight a hairdo, it could last for weeks. I didn't know how thick hair could be until I grew up and felt its soft density supporting my chin as we two slept.

I wanted to see her as different, that little girl. I remember her wearing pink and suddenly throwing up all of Pacific Ocean Park out of her rollercoastered gut, the puddle of stink and sickness one person away from me. That wasn't me. That was someone else's guts lying in a lumpy grey puddle in the line to the "Wild Ride." An hour later, getting off the same roller coaster, I fought desperately to keep down the cheap spaghetti dinner rolling around in my stomach, rising in my throat. I didn't want to be that human, that exposed, that dark.

There was a time when I truly believed I could never live without Black women in my life. And then I learned how—how to forget uptown city buses, her fedora-feathered dreads, her femme fatality sliding up next to me. We peer out onto street-soaked Harlem. She, small-town-colored-girl-import; me, "Spanish." But somehow we managed to make home in Harlem, her talking the talk, in girlsclubsboysclubs, with girls&boys always eyeing us, envying. Or so we imagined.

I imagined I could never live without that. That her. That life. But then I did learn to live without and then Audre died and I remembered that biography denied me. I dial New York, hear my name echoed back to me familiar. "We were so young," my sister says. And Black, a decade ago blackfamilia. Audre was our dark womanhood wrapped around dark womanhood in subways and on street corners, kissing under rain-soaked umbrellas, in the basement of a mid-town Church where we plotted coloredgirl revolution. I had a Black family once and what happened to that? Like my Mexican childhood, my Puerto Rican dreams, my white forgetfulness. What happened to all those women I laid and made history with?

·····

You Wanted a Real Mexican, You Got It

I can't write of pink-nippled breasts
how I've looked so harshly at my own,
how I grow in the delight of their darkening
how once a black-nippled Mexican lover

threw up my shirt exposed
my nipples and they all laughed
at their pathetic rose-colored softness

they all laughed and I grew
dark in my anger and resolve

The first colored woman I slept with wasn't colored at all but darker than me in *her* anger, in *her* resolve. And I tasted on her immigrant tongue resting speechless upon mine a sister of tragic dimension. How she envied me my education, my seamless face, my freedom. The taste was bitter and mother-Mexican familiar. I wanted more...

My first Chicana lover was the smoothness of the clay pots she dragged from home to home, making home out of anything, stolen milk crates, heavy tamales of woolen Indian blankets. She was a childless woman like me, a woman, as Don Juan describes it, 'without holes in her body'. Still, like those Mexican pots, she had a wide open mouth, ready to devour everything surrounding her. This was lesbian, I discovered. And I had never been so in love...

I thought I met a lesbian once, an Indian woman from the south of Oaxaca who sat three tables away from us at a club in the capital city. As the salsa band plays, I watch the woman in a short mannish haircut watch us, a table of U.S. Latinas, as Sabrina takes her girlfriend out to dance. When they return to the table, the waiter brings us another round, courtesy of the woman three tables away. We invite her to join us. She is already drunk and her tears well up and flow down effortlessly as she recounts to my comadre, Myrtha, the story of her passage here to this city of ricos and government officials and poverty. She speaks of a recent death, the murder of a family member. And with the same despair, she speaks of the sudden cutting of her trenza. A government program had brought her here, hundreds of miles away from her village, and filled her pockets with pesos and her belly with mescal. She cries, and eyeing Sabrina's Indian trenza and Mixteca features, keeps wanting to understand who we all were. We try to explain, but she only cries all the more as the full moon passes into view through the zócalo window. She tells us that at that very moment she is missing her village's ceremonia to the moon. I mention the moon's Indian name "Coyolxauhqui." She stares at me. It is the first time she has looked at me all evening. "How do you know that?" she asks. "You are white." And I look over to Myrtha whose watery eyes have held the woman's for over an hour. We smile, sadly. "She's right," I say later. "In her world, I'm just white."

It was Myrtha who told me on a particularly gloomy Berkeley afternoon, "You don't know what it feels like to always be perceived as 'Third World,' to see in everybody's eyes that disdain, that desprecio." And yet, we move around these ancient Mexican sites from Palenque to Monte Albán like long lost sister-companions. Una puertorriqueña y una chicana, we speak in a wordless code to each other. We are without nationality in the deepest sense, even though they only ask me and the Germans for passports on this bus full of Mexicanos and Myrtha. She doesn't mention it, her hand resting on mine. Neither do I.

And suddenly I remember the lover I had left, weeks earlier, on the sandy streets of a Mexican beach town, and the one distinct time I made love with her and shook. Shook from the tequila still poisoning my veins, shook from how boldly her americaneyes stripped me of my Chicana cultural bravado, shook from how naked I felt. And I remember vaguely, because I was so drunk, the trip across to the island, her holding my back as I threw up in a bag. I remember her getting us to the hotel in a cab. I remember her hand always guiding my back, and I remember again throwing up all that bitterness, all that self-hatred, all that disgust at my whiteness, my hunger to be part of that memory, that México. And I called her "sister," too. With a voice I use only for my own blood-sister's name, as I worked my hand and tongue inside of her, trying to find a place to rest all that homesickness.

In 1986, I wrote a play in which a Mexican woman says of her young Chicana lover, *"Sometimes I think with me that she only wanted to feel herself so much a woman that she would no longer be hungry for one."* Today in my own voice I would add, "I only wanted to feel myself so much a *Mexican...*" But I am always hungry and always shamed by my hunger for the Mexican woman I miss in myself.

> *I would have left sooner if it hadn't been for the smell of albóndigas in her kitchen, the sticky desert taste of nopalito behind her ears, the texture of that thick rope of hemp hair I twisted into my fist, holding her hamaca and swaying beneath me.*

> *I would have left her if her Spanish had been less than perfectly provincial, her repertoire of rancheras lacking, her knowledge of brujería anything but respectfully re-strained.*

> *I would have left her for a woman less Mexican if México had not been so forgotten in me. Instead I stayed and stayed and stayed until México no longer mattered*

*so much, became an island thoroughly remote and un-
reachable, grew dim in my explorer's imagination.*

I write the word "explorer" and shudder at the image it evokes,
of some sixteenth-century iron-clad conquistador or beaver-capped
Northwest trapper. I am both the "explorer" and the "Indígena."
Most Mexicans can claim the same, but my claim is more "explorer"
than not. And yes, most days I am deathly ashamed. But of what,
exactly? My white family was kept distant from me, not because of
its conquests, but because of its failures.

.....

She Won't Let Go

I grew up judging the white side of my family very cruelly. Our
one family of white cousins were abandoned children, fed from
giant-sized peanut butter jars, while we Mexican cousins ate home-
made warm tortillas with a clean embroidered tablecloth under our
elbows. There was the story one of those white cousins told of how
her mother—my aunt, my Father's only sister—would punish her
by locking her in a room where she had to piss and shit in coffee
cans. And I remember my sister at five, after a week's stay at my
aunt's house, never wanting to return; she became frightened of the
dark, of closed closet doors.

Many years later, after having not seen my aunt for nearly twenty
years, we meet at a Chinese restaurant. She has just received word
that she may have cancer. She fears she is dying and wants to repair
any damages done. We are not her children. We have nothing to forgive
in her, except her twenty-year absence. I am the last to arrive at the
restaurant. My mother, father, sister, and she have already ordered

drinks and appetizers. As I enter, I spot her first. She looks as I remembered her, only a little older, thicker, tougher. But she was always tough, tougher than her brother, the protected one. She reminds me of a dyke. She is not a dyke, but sees something queer in me as I approach the table smiling. "You're your grandma Hallie, " she says to me after the second drink. "You've got her spirit. Did you know that?" No, I didn't know that any more than I knew the woman herself. But I am hungry to know, as my sister is. So, the stories begin...stories that had been censored by my father. Stories of my French grandma's wild ways, her five marriages, the last to a homosexual, her adopted daughter never to be heard from again. My grandma was a wild woman in a white Cadillac with white skin and white bleached hair. But to my five-year-old mind, she was merely a strange wrinkled lady with long red painted fingernails that she used like a tortilla to push her food onto her fork. She was white, and therefore foreign. And now, over a generation later, her daughter tells me I was made in her likeness. Later, I learn of the WPA and my grandmother's vaudeville days; I learn to put the pieces together. She was an independent woman, my white grandma, a woman with an artist's hunger for love and limelight.

Once my aunt appeared to me in a dream. I cannot see her face, because she stands behind me, holding me, her arms around me like a straightjacket. I panic. She won't let go. I wake up, heart pounding. In another dream, my aunt is a waitress slapping hash onto a grill and plates onto customers' tables. My Mexican aunts and my mother are nearby. They sit hunched around a low table. They are whispering secrets. They appear very dark, like brujas. This gathering is a holy coven. I stand between this circle of witches and my working-class aunt. She throws a hand on her hip, wipes her brow with the back of the other. "These Mexicans," she says, "are so damn crazy!" My cousin David appears. He is brown and beautiful, indifferent to the world of women around him. He does not have to choose. He remains aloof and elegant in his Mexican masculinity. He does not sweat. I envy him.

She will not let go. My aunt died this year, not of the cancer she had feared ten years ago, but of a stroke. She died quietly and tragically a few months after she had retired from forty-plus years working as a nurse and supporting seven children who have known drugs and alcoholism and gun-shot wounds more intimately than any of us Mexicans. My girl-cousin, the one who suffered those early "lock-ups" was the one who was at her side, holding her mother's square freckled hand (my father's hand) until the moment of her passing.

.....

"What's a 'Betty'?" I ask. We are coming out of the theatre, out from the world of Spike Lee's *X*. The images still reel inside me: 1940s Black Boston strutting zoot suits and conks; Harlem in the hopping fifties and heady sixties; a beautiful Denzel Washington, with smoked red hair, speaking revolution, "By any means necessary." In the congregation hall of Black Muslims, the women are draped nun-like in white; the men are a stolid block of dark suits. A banner waves above their heads: "Our women are our most valuable property." I cringe at the word, "property," as I do at the blue-black prison scene where Malcolm Little swears off the "white man's swine" and the "white man's women" in the same breath.

And the word "Betty" comes to mind, I don't know why. My companion answers, "She's a 'bimbo', a Black man's white woman. She's considered 'trash' by everyone—Black *and* white—cuz, the thinking goes, why would a woman who really had somethin' going for herself 'slum it' with a Black man." "That's pretty ugly on all counts," I say. Still, I push her away from me that night, that white away from me. *But she will not let go.*

My white aunt comes to visit me as all the women in my family have, uninvited through my bedroom door. She will stay until she is given the respect due her. She will stay until she has changed from a faceless entity straightjacketing my every movement into a woman of real flesh and bones and name. My aunt's name is Barbara and I am here to make peace with her in the white women I love, in the white woman I am. All those "Bettys," that "trash," that working-class whitegirl I learned to fear on the "other" side of the family, on the "other" side of me.

.....

Talkin' Breed Talk

Some of my mixed-blood friends have had "Bettys" for mothers. Their task is a harder one, I think—to carve out an identity as a "colored" woman without a colored woman to look to. I wrote in 1983, "My brother's sex was white, mine brown." I still believe that to my core. But regardless of how the dice were tossed and what series of accidents put our two parents—one white and one colored—together, we, their offspring, have had to choose who we are in racist Amerika.

It is best for them (Anglos) when we (Chicano/as) are light-skinned, but better still when Chicano/as are half-white and half-Chicano/a. That places half-breeds closer to Anglo language and culture. But these false privileges many recognize for what they are, a token, a maldición.

— Emma Pérez,
"Sexuality and Discourse: Notes from a Chicana Survivor"

Emma's got it right. In the "choice" resides the curse, the "maldición." There is no denying that this güera-face has often secured my safe passage through the minefields of Amerikan racism. *If my thoughts could color my flesh, how dark I would turn.* But people can't read your mind, they read your color, they read your womanhood, they read the women you're with. They read your walk and talk. And then the privileges begin to wane and the choices become more limited, more evident. I think that is why I have always hated the terms "biracial" and "bisexual." They are passive terms, without political bite. They don't choose. They don't make a decision. They are a declaration not of identity, but of biology, of sexual practice. They say nothing about where one really stands. And as long as injustice prevails, we do not have the luxury of calling ourselves either.

Call me breed. Call me trash. Call me spic greaser beaner dyke jota bulldagger. Call me something meant to set me apart from you and I will know who I am. Do not call me "sister." I am not yours.

Do I write this to my brother who has chosen, against me, who he will be in this lifetime? He does not perceive his white manhood as a choice. To him it is the natural evolution of a light-skinned mixed-blood son of a white man. But Jacobo doesn't feel this way, Tim doesn't feel this way, Mekaya doesn't feel this way—all these breed-boys ever loyal to the dark side of their mestizaje. The blondest of the bunch writes it blue-veined into his skin: *¡Viva la Raza!* A life-long mark of identity, of loyalty to his mother's and to his own people.

Only my sister understands. She tells me, "nobody I know talks about this, Ceci, about being mixed." Nobody else has to—prove who they are, prove who they aren't. Of our 100-plus cousins, she and I are the only ones working with la Raza, working to maintain that conexión under the constant threat of denial. I know full well that my mestizaje— my breed blood—is the catalyst of my activism and my art. I have tasted assimilation and it is bitter on my tongue. Had I been born a full-blood Mexican, I sometimes wonder whether I would have struggled so hard to stay a part of la raza.

.....

18 February 1990: Sueño

I see in the distance, a herd of calf-children traveling in packs with their white lesbian mothers. They are half-animal, half-human. They are goat-people, young calves with the expressions of injured children. One has the buttocks of a human, but it is fur-covered like an animal. They are me.

After they pass, I approach a table where one of the mothers is selling wares. I am eating cheese and she tells me I must stand away from the table, something about the mixing of elements (the cheese I am eating with what she is selling). I inquire about the half-breed children. She informs me that there is one father for all of them and they have turned out this way due to a mixing of bloods—too many with one father.

I want to chastise the women for their irresponsibility, but the thought passes through my mind that possibly there is another meaning here, inside the bodies of these deformed ones. The creation of a new species (half-human / half-animal). Maybe they are the hope of the future, these mixed beings who will bridge a world of opposition, re-unite the human with the natural world.

And I am not alone in this dreaming. Recently, a mixed-blood Indian sister told me of her dream like mine. In it she is raped by a lion and becomes pregnant. She is outraged until she realizes that she is the one named to bear the new species—half-beast half-she. She tells me how much the dream disturbed her. "I don't want to be the fuckin' virgin mary of the next generation." "Me neither, " I say. "Me neither."

As mixed-blood women, we are the hybrid seed she carried in the dream and the mothers of a new generation. We are the products of rape and the creators of a new breed. We are Malinche's children and the new Malinches of the 21st century. We are talkin' breed talk when the whole world's turning breed at unprecedented rates, [*] when Third and Fourth and First Worlds are collapsing into one another. But make no mistake, there still is the Rapist Father and he is white and the Violated Mother and she is not. In spite of the personal stories to the contrary, the political conditions of miscegenation, to this day, occur within the larger framework of a white supremacist society. And miscegenation's children wrestle, in one way or another, with the consequences.

I am not that rare breed of mixed-blood person, a Jean Toomer, who writes, as Alice Walker said of *Cane*, "to memorialize a culture he thought was dying." I am that raging breed of mixed-blood person

---

[*]Although this essay concerns my personal experience of mixed parentage—one white and one of color—the "21st century mestizo" is increasingly born of two parents of color of different races and/or ethnicities.

who writes to defend a culture that I know is being killed. I am of that endangered culture and of that murderous race, but I am loyal only to one. My mother culture, my mother land, my mother tongue, further back than even she can remember.

My father said it himself, speaking of the whiteman, "We are our own worst enemies." I don't betray my whitefather, that gentle man, in writing this. I live up to the mixed-raced legacy his people have betrothed to me.

.....

Remembering Navajo Nation

July 22, 1992

I have witnessed speechless beauty, this nation of Diné. My insignificance enters me amid the antiquity of these red rock canyons. I have no desire to return or go forward. There is nowhere to arrive, only this journeying....

I remember Phoenix. My cousin, Rudy, and my Tía Lupe: that dying breed of Mexican cowboy and his mother. My aunt of 83 years is speechless like me. She can't recall English *or* Spanish words, just can't seem to bring them to the surface of her tongue. The facts: dates, names, places. She falters..."Desde que murió mi viejo...," forgetting who *is* her "viejo." At times her son, forty years younger, takes on that old indio's shape and voice. She looks to him to finish her lines. He waits. She suffers. Rainclouds form over Navajo Nation. The sky darkens. We wait. *The sun will break through these clouds.*

My companion mistakenly keeps calling Rudy my "brother," although he is a brother of sorts. More than my own. The queer son, like me, desperately clinging to history. The family anthropologist searching out raíces from the bowels of Mission churches in a Sonora that once hardly knew the word "gringo."

We are the childless ones, he and I. I find a brother in the pasión he exudes when pulling out death certificates and reproduced photos of what could be Indian, could be Arabe, could be "old country" great-great-grandmothers. He names them: Refugia, Paula, Victoria, braids stretched across seamless foreheads, skin stretched across chiseled cheekbones, hazel eyes buried into them. Conversing with my cousin, I search his words, his excited moving mouth. The Spanish surnames spill from his tongue...Figueroa, Mendibles, Rodríguez...I swallow, hesitate. I ask, "And the Indians?...Did you find out anything about our Indian blood?" "Oh there must have been some," he says. But no mention, no unnamed bisabuelo. Still, the dark faces appear and disappear in photographs with no native claim, no name.

.....

The road is red in Arizona. A river of red clay. I am surrounded by red and spin it green in poetic imagination. What are the names of these trees that hover like sentinels by the river's weed banks? This is Chimayó clay water that flows all the way from Nuevo México, Guatemala. This is Quiché clay. I remember Elena's words, "You have so much air, Ceci. Walk the earth with bare feet. Feel the ground."

I remove my shoes. I walk. I want this mud to stain me red from the soles up. My toes turn purple with the chill of the creek, bleed rose red into the clay.

No wonder you became a potter, a worker of clay,
a sculptor.
No wonder you studied how to shape your hands
into forms these canón walls etch
into the raingodskies.
Half-breed sister, half-sister, no wonder.

We are a mongrel nation, and yet this ground is testimony to the purity of the sacred. Water and earth blend, turn the river mud red, and it refreshes no less through the open pores of flesh and palm. Open palm.

When did our real ancestors arrive here?
Before Olmec heads and Mayan gods?
Before gods?

I am a trespasser. I do not need signs to remind me. My immigrant blood is a stain I carry in the fading of my flesh each winter. But I am made of clay. All our ancestors know this. It is no myth, but wholly evident in the slow dissolving of my skin into the red road of this river. *Where will you take me, immigrant and orphaned?*

All is familia: ancestor and future generations. The tree branches out, bears fruit. The canón grows dark and I dream of dying. Not violence, but a slow and peaceful return to the river.

For my sister, Jo Ann

The Last Generation

It's the land.
You cannot own the land.
The land owns you.
– sung by Dolores Keane
from "Solid Ground"

Meditation

the third eye

never cries

it knows.

I Don't Know the Protocol

I fly along these backroads. I want to keep consuming miles under the spin and bump of my tires. I don't ever want to arrive...anywhere. But I stop when I see the stiff hide of bones and meat. I pull over onto the gravel that shoulders a frost-grey pasture.

As I approach the deer, I already know she has been dead since nightfall. Dawn found her this way, stonestill, no trace of blood, but there is the telltale foam spilling from her lengthened tongue. Is it a tongue or a piece of raw meat she has regurgitated?

I am afraid to look at the face of her recent, so recent, death. Why am I afraid? I don't know the protocol. I have only read about this in books. I have only heard about tobacco and offerings to deer who sacrifice themselves to the hunt. This reckless hunter abandoned her, did not consume her flesh. Her flesh must be so bitter. Are all prey turned bitter by the bullet, the speeding car, the butcher's hatchet?

I know she is wiser than I. I know she is no dumb animal. I pray stupidly, wafting her with sage smoke, sprinkling tobacco at hoofs, forehead, foaming mouth. I don't know the protocol and I wonder if my actions are a mockery to a knowledge missing from me now.

But I pray for her and all of her kind who will be offered up to this "season" of white Texans in Amerikan-made pickup trucks, rifles riding horizontal behind their heads, deer bleeding out of open-bed U-Hauls. The hunters congregate in packs like animals. But unlike animals, they plot, create ritual, drink coffee, eat donuts, pat each other's flannel-covered shoulders, and think they will live forever.

Rattle and flute sounds rise up from the dashboard. It is a "Yaqui Deer Dance." I don't know why I chose it, why it called me from the shelf in San Anto, why I don't know where tobacco belongs on a dead deer.

Madre

En este Día de los Muertos
rezo no solo para los muertos
de ayer
sino para los muertos
de mañana
de quienes yo también
seré miembro,

Madre.

Our Lady of the Cannery Workers

for Celia Rodríguez

In June 1992 in Watsonville, California, a U.S.-Mexican town of cannery and agricultural workers, a woman reported that la virgen maría had appeared to her near the county park lake where her son had drowned a few years earlier. Nearby, a tree took on the Virgin's form in its bark.

Returning from Watsonville
the road, a forest of apparitions
the Mother Creator
in every Standing
Sequoia
every Virgin Forest.

Ehécatl
follows me
reminds me to listen
to the stillness
observe
her subtle and violent
appearance
in pine-scented breezes
copal dancing smoke
in icy san francisco winds
whipping through open bedroom
windows, sudden slamming

doors: *did she enter just then?*
was she taking leave
of her senses?

she, the pinwheel descent
of an aging
oak
leaf

Is this the same tree
sheltered beneath the giant
umbrella of sequoia
that bears the shape of Guadalupe
in its breast? A tattoo
emblazoned into the scaling bark flesh
that same slight inclination
of shrouded head, the same
copper rose shade
imprinted on the tela
of Juan Diego's prayer?

Tonantzín
te traigo flores.

Pilgrims hold up mirrors to the sun.
Beams of light ricochet in all directions.
Earthmother colors
illuminate
coastal gloom,
factory shut-downs

migra raids.

Ahora, ¿la ves?
Sí.
Dios te salve
María.

Juanita vestida de blanco
advises the faithful,
"Let go de su coraje."
I thread
my angry fingers
through the chain link
a sagging fortress
of protection.
My swollen knuckles
woven into the rusting wire
like rosary beads
of pink, turquoise-colored glass
carved pine wood
draped from curling polaroids.
Family prayers hang
by a thread
of christmas ribbon.

There is one who refuses
to pray the catholic words
buries small ties
of tobacco at the four corners
she is Diego's living relative

her anger, righteous
and unforgiving.

If la virgen appeared to me,
what would she look like?
Not cannery worker
but pintora?

Sequoia Virgen
I see you in every crevice
of your burnt red flesh
vagina openings split
into two thick thighs
of female eruption.

you grow old and tall
you fall

you turn to seed.

Queer Aztlán: the Re-formation of Chicano Tribe

How will our lands be free if our bodies aren't?
— Ricardo Bracho

At the height of the Chicano Movement in 1968, I was a closeted, light-skinned, mixed-blood Mexican-American, disguised in my father's English last name. Since I seldom opened my mouth, few people questioned my Anglo credentials. But my eyes were open and thirsty and drank in images of students my age, of vatos and viejitas, who could have primos, or tíos, or abuelitas raising their collective fists into a smoggy East Los Angeles skyline. Although I could not express how at the time, I knew I had a place in that

Movement that was spilling out of barrio high schools and onto police-barricaded streets just ten minutes from my tree-lined working-class neighborhood in San Gabriel. What I didn't know then was that it would take me another ten years to fully traverse that ten-minute drive and to bring all the parts of me—Chicana, lesbiana, half-breed, and poeta—to the revolution, wherever it was.*

My real politicization began, not through the Chicano Movement, but through the bold recognition of my lesbianism. Coming to terms with that fact meant the radical re-structuring of everything I thought I held sacred. It meant acting on my woman-centered desire and against anything that stood in its way, including my Church, my family, and my "country." It meant acting in spite of the fact that I had learned from my Mexican culture and the dominant culture that my womanhood was, if not despised, certainly deficient and hardly worth the loving of another woman in bed. But act I did, because not acting would have meant my death by despair.

That was twenty years ago. In those twenty years I traversed territory that extends well beyond the ten-minute trip between East Los Angeles and San Gabriel. In those twenty years, I experienced the racism of the Women's Movement, the elitism of the Gay and Lesbian Movement, the homophobia and sexism of the Chicano Movement, and the benign cultural imperialism of the Latin American Solidarity Movement. I also witnessed the emergence of a national

*An earlier version of this essay was first presented at the First National LLEGO (Latino/a Lesbian and Gay Organization) Conference in Houston, Texas, on May 22, 1992. A later version was presented at a Quincentenary Conference at the University of Texas in Austin on October 31, 1992.

Chicana feminist consciousness and a literature, art, and activism to support it. I've seen the growth of a lesbian-of-color movement, the founding of an independent national Latino/a lesbian and gay men's organization, and the flourishing of Indigenous people's international campaigns for human and land rights.

A quarter of a century after those school walk-outs in 1968, I can write, without reservation, that I have found a sense of place among la Chicanada. It is not always a safe place, but it is unequivocally the original familial place from which I am compelled to write, which I reach toward in my audiences, and which serves as my source of inspiration, voice, and lucha. How we Chicanos define that struggle has always been the subject of debate and is ultimately the subject of this essay.

.....

"Queer Aztlán" had been forming in my mind for over three years and began to take concrete shape a year ago in a conversation with poet Ricardo Bracho. We discussed the limitations of "Queer Nation," whose leather-jacketed, shaved-headed white radicals and accompanying anglo-centricity were an "alien-nation" to most lesbians and gay men of color. We also spoke of Chicano Nationalism, which never accepted openly gay men and lesbians among its ranks. Ricardo half-jokingly concluded, "What we need, Cherríe, is a 'Queer Aztlán.' " Of course. A Chicano homeland that could embrace *all* its people, including its jotería.[*]

* Chicano term for "queer" folk.

Everything I read these days tells me that the Chicano Movement is dead. In Earl Shorris' *Latinos*, the Anglo author insists that the Chicano *him*self is dead. He writes, "The Chicano generation began in the late 1960s and lasted about six or eight years, dying slowly through the seventies." He goes on to say that Chicanismo has been reduced to no more than a "handshake practiced by middle-aged men." Chicano sociologists seem to be suggesting the same when they tell us that by the third generation, the majority of Chicanos have lost their Spanish fluency, and nearly a third have married non-Chicanos and have moved out of the Chicano community. Were immigration from México to stop, they say, Chicanos could be virtually indistinguishable from the rest of the population within a few generations. My nieces and nephews are living testimony to these faceless facts.

I mourn the dissolution of an active Chicano Movement possibly more strongly than my generational counterparts because during its "classic period," I was unable to act publicly. But more deeply, I mourn it because its ghost haunts me daily in the blonde hair of my sister's children, the gradual hispanicization of Chicano students, the senselessness of barrio violence, and the poisoning of la frontera from Tijuana to Tejas. In 1992, we have no organized national movement to respond to our losses. For me, "El Movimiento" has never been a thing of the past, it has retreated into subterranean uncontaminated soils awaiting resurrection in a "queerer," more feminist generation.

What was right about Chicano Nationalism was its commitment to preserving the integrity of the Chicano people. A generation ago, there were cultural, economic, and political programs to develop Chicano consciousness, autonomy, and self-determination. What was wrong about Chicano Nationalism was its institutionalized heterosexism, its inbred machismo, and its lack of a cohesive national political strategy.[*]

Over the years, I have witnessed plenty of progressive nationalisms: Chicano nationalism, Black nationalism, Puerto Rican Independence (still viable as evidenced in the recent mass protest on the Island against the establishment of English as an official language), the "Lesbian Nation" and its lesbian separatist movement, and, of course, the most recent "Queer Nation." What I admired about each was its righteous radicalism, its unabashed anti-assimilationism, and its rebeldía. I recognize the dangers of nationalism as a strategy for political change. Its tendency toward separatism can run dangerously close to biological determinism and a kind of fascism. We are all horrified by the concentration and rape camps in Bosnia, falsely justified by the Serbian call for "ethnic cleansing." We are bitterly sobered by the nazism espoused by Pat Buchanan at the 1992 Republican Convention in which only heterosexual white middle-class voting Amerikans have the right to citizenship and heaven. Over and over again we are reminded that sex and race do not define a person's politics. Margaret Thatcher is a woman and enforces the policies of the Imperial whiteman and Clarence Thomas is Black and follows suit. But it is historically evident that the female body, like the Chicano people, has been colonized. And any movement to decolonize them must be culturally and sexually specific.

---

[*]To this day, there are still pockets of Chicano nationalists—mostly artists, poets, and cultural workers—who continue to work on a local and regional level.

Chicanos are an occupied nation within a nation, and women and women's sexuality are occupied within Chicano nation. If women's bodies and those of men and women who transgress their gender roles have been historically regarded as territories to be conquered, they are also territories to be liberated. Feminism has taught us this. The nationalism I seek is one that decolonizes the brown and female body as it decolonizes the brown and female earth. It is a new nationalism in which la Chicana Indígena stands at the center, and heterosexism and homophobia are no longer the cultural order of the day. I cling to the word "nation" because without the specific naming of the nation, the nation will be lost (as when feminism is reduced to humanism, the woman is subsumed). Let us retain our radical naming but expand it to meet a broader and wiser revolution.

.....

Tierra Sagrada: The Roots of a Revolution

Aztlán. I don't remember when I first heard the word, but I remember it took my heart by surprise to learn of that place—that "sacred landscape" wholly evident en las playas, los llanos, y en las montañas of the North American Southwest. A terrain that I did not completely comprehend at first, but that I continue to try, in my own small way, to fully inhabit and make habitable for its Chicano citizens.

Aztlán gave language to a nameless anhelo inside me. To me, it was never a masculine notion. It had nothing to do with the Aztecs and everything to do with Mexican birds, Mexican beaches, and

Mexican babies right here in Califas. I remember once driving through Anza Borrego desert, just east of San Diego, my VW van whipping around corners, climbing. The tape deck set at full blast, every window open, bandana around my forehead. And I think, *this is México, Raza territory,* as I belt out the refrain...

> *"Marieta, no seas coqueta*
> *porque los hombres son muy malos*
> *prometen muchos regalos*
> *y lo que dan son puro palos..."*

That day I claimed that land in the spin of the worn-out tape, the spin of my balding tires, and the spin of my mind. And just as I wrapped around a rubber-burning curve, I saw it: **"A-Z-T-L-A-N,"** in granite-sized letters etched into the face of the mountainside. Of course, I hadn't been the first. Some other Chicano came this way, too, saw what I saw, felt what I felt. Enough to put a name to it. *Aztlán. Tierra sagrada.*

A term Náhuatl in root, Aztlán was that historical/mythical land where one set of Indian forebears, the Aztecs, were said to have resided 1,000 years ago. Located in the U.S. Southwest, Aztlán fueled a nationalist struggle twenty years ago, which encompassed much of the pueblo Chicano from Chicago to the borders of Chihuahua. In the late sixties and early seventies, Chicano nationalism meant the right to control our own resources, language, and cultural traditions, rights guaranteed us by the Treaty of Guadalupe Hidalgo signed in 1848 when the Southwest was "annexed" to the United States at the end of the Mexican-American War. At its most radical, Chicano nationalism expressed itself in militant action. In the mid-1960s, Reies López Tijerina entered a campaign against the

Department of the Interior to reclaim land grants for New Mexicans, resulting in his eventual imprisonment. In 1968, nearly 10,000 Chicano students walked out of their high schools to protest the lack of quality education in Los Angeles barrio schools. The same period also saw the rise of the Brown Berets, a para-military style youth organization regularly harassed by law enforcement agencies throughout the Southwest. These are highlights in Chicano Movement history. To most, however, El Movimiento, practically applied, simply meant fair and equitable representation on the city council, in the union halls, and on the school board.

I've often wondered why Chicano nationalism never really sustained the same level of militancy witnessed in the Puerto Rican, Black, and Native American Movements. Certainly violence, especially police violence, was visited upon Chicanos in response to our public protests, the murder of journalist Rubén Salazar during the National Chicano Moratorium of 1970 being the most noted instance. And like other liberation movements, the Chicano movement had its share of FBI infiltrators.

In 1969, El Plan de Aztlán was drawn up at the First Annual Chicano Youth Conference in Denver, Colorado, calling for a Chicano program of economic self-determination, self-defense, and land reclamation, and including an autonomous taxation and judicial system. By the mid-1970s, such radical plans had gradually eroded in the face of a formidable opponent—the United States government—and Chicano nationalism as a political strategy began to express itself more in the cultural arena than in direct militant confrontation with the government.

Another reason for the brevity of a unified militant movement may be the heterogeneity of the Chicano population. Chicanos are not easily organized as a racial/political entity. Is our land the

México of today or the México of a century and a half ago, covering thousands of miles of what is now the Southwestern United States? Unlike the island of Puerto Rico whose "homeland" is clearly defined by ocean on all sides, Aztlán at times seems more *meta*physical than physical territory.

As a mestizo people living in the United States, our relationship to this country has been ambivalent at best. Our birth certificates since the invasion of Aztlán identify us as white. Our treatment by Anglo-Americans brand us "colored." In the history of African Americans, when the white slaveowner raped a Black woman, the mixed-blood offspring inherited the mother's enslaved status. Over a century later, mixed-raced African Americans overwhelmingly identify as Black, not as mixed-blood. But the history of Mexicans/Chicanos follows a different pattern. The "Spanish-American" Conquest was secured through rape, intermarriage, the African slave trade, and the spread of Catholicism and disease. It gave birth to a third "mestizo" race that included Indian, African, and European blood. During colonial times, "Spanish-America" maintained a rigid and elaborate caste system that privileged the pure-blood Spaniard and his children over the mestizo. The pure blood indio and africano remained on the bottom rungs of society. The remnants of such class/race stratification are still evident throughout Latin America.

Chicano Nation is a mestizo nation conceived in a double-rape: first, by the Spanish and then by the Gringo. In the mid-19th century, Anglo-America took possession of one-third of México's territory. A new English-speaking oppressor assumed control over the Spanish, Mestizo, and Indian people inhabiting those lands. There was no denying that the United States had stolen Aztlán from México, but it had been initially stolen from the Indians by the

Spanish some 300 years earlier. To make alliances with other nationalist struggles taking place throughout the country in the late sixties, there was no room for Chicano ambivalence about being Indians, for it was our Indian blood and history of resistance against both Spanish and Anglo invaders that made us rightful inheritors of Aztlán. After centuries of discrimination against our Indian-ness, which forced mestizos into denial, many Mexican-Americans found the sudden affirmation of our indigenismo difficult to accept. And yet the Chicano Indigenous movement was not without historical precedence. Little more than fifty years earlier, México witnessed a campesino- and Indian-led agrarian and labor movement spreading into the Southwest that had the potential of eclipsing the Russian Revolution in its vision. Political corruption, of course, followed. Today, the pending Free Trade Agreement with the United States and Canada marks the ultimate betrayal of the Mexican revolution: the final surrender of the Mexican people's sovereign rights to land and livelihood.

.....

Radicalization among people of Mexican ancestry in this country most often occurs when the Mexican ceases to be a Mexican and becomes a Chicano. I have observed this in my Chicano Studies students, (first, second, and third generation, some of whose families are indigenous to Aztlán) from the barrios of East Los Angeles, Fresno, and all the neighboring Central Valley towns of California— Selma, Visalia, Sanger, the barrios of Oakland, Sanjo, etc. They are the ones most often in protest, draping their bodies in front of freeway on-ramps and trans-bay bridges, blocking entrances to University administration buildings. They are the ones who, like their Black, Asian, and Native American counterparts, doubt the "American dream" because even if *they* got to UC Berkeley, their brother is still on crack in Boyle Heights, their sister had three kids before she's twenty, and *sorry but they can't finish the last week of the semester cuz Tío Ignacio just got shot in front of a liquor store.* My working-class and middle-class Mexican immigrant students,[*] on the other hand, have not yet had their self-esteem nor that of their parents and grandparents worn away by North American racism. For them, the "American dream" still looms as a possibility on the horizon. Their Mexican pride sustains them through the daily assaults on their intelligence, integrity, and humanity. They maintain a determined individualism and their families still dream of returning home one day.

A new generation of future Chicanos arrives everyday with every Mexican immigrant. Some may find their American dream and forget their origins, but the majority of México's descendants soon comprehend the political meaning of the disparity between their lives and those of the gringo. Certainly the Mexican women cannery workers of Watsonville who maintained a two-year victorious strike against Green Giant in the mid-eighties, and farm workers organized by César Chávez's UFW in the late sixties and early seventies are testimony to the political militancy of the Mexican immigrant worker. More recently, there are the examples of the Mothers of East Los Angeles and the women of Kettleman City who

---

[*]UC Berkeley's Chicano/Latino immigrant students have not generally encountered the same degree of poverty and exploitation experienced by undocumented Mexican and Central American immigrants.

have organized against the toxic contamination proposed for their communities. In the process, the Mexicana becomes a Chicana (or at least a Mechicana); that is, she becomes a citizen of this country, not by virtue of a green card, but by virtue of the collective voice she assumes in staking her claim to this land and its resources.

.....

Plumas Planchadas: The De-formation of the Movement

> With our heart in our hands and our hands in the soil,
> we declare the independence of our mestizo nation.
> —"El Plan Espiritual de Aztlán"

El Movimiento did not die out in the seventies, as most of its critics claim; it was only deformed by the machismo and homophobia of that era and coopted by "hispanicization" of the eighties.[*] In reaction against Anglo-America's emasculation of Chicano men, the male-dominated Chicano Movement embraced the most patriarchal aspects of its Mexican heritage. For a generation, nationalist leaders used a kind of "selective memory," drawing exclusively from those aspects of Mexican and Native cultures that served the interests of male heterosexuals. At times, they took the worst of Mexican machismo and Aztec warrior bravado, combined it with some of the most oppressive male-conceived

---

[*]Further discussion of the "hispanicization" of the U.S. Latino can be found in the essay, "Art in América con Acento" in this collection.

idealizations of "traditional" Mexican womanhood and called that
cultural integrity. They subscribed to a machista view of women, based
on the centuries-old virgin-whore paradigm of la Virgen de Guadalupe
and Malintzin Tenepal. Guadalupe represented the Mexican ideal of
"la madre sufrida," the long-suffering desexualized Indian mother, and
Malinche was "la chingada," sexually stigmatized by her transgression
of "sleeping with the enemy," Hernán Cortez. Deemed traitor by
Mexican tradition, the figure of Malinche was invoked to keep
Movimiento women silent, sexually passive, and "Indian" in the colonial sense of the word.

The preservation of the Chicano familia became the
Movimiento's mandate and within this constricted "familia" structure, Chicano políticos ensured that the patriarchal father figure
remained in charge both in their private and political lives.[*] Women
were, at most, allowed to serve as modern-day "Adelitas," performing the "three fs" as a Chicana colleague calls them: "feeding,
fighting, and fucking." In the name of this "culturally correct"
familia, certain topics were censored both in cultural and political

[*]The twenty-five-year-old Chicano Teatro Movement is an apt example.
Initiated by Luis Valdez' Teatro Campesino, the teatro movement has
been notorious for its male dominance even within its so-called collective structures. Over eighty percent of the Chicano Theatres across the
country are directed by men. No affirmative-action policies have been
instituted to encourage the development of Chicana playwrights, tech-
nicians, or directors. In recent years, however, there has been some
progress in this area with the production of a handful of Chicana
playwrights, including Josefina Lopez, Evelina Fernández, Edit
Villareal, and this author. To this day, gay and lesbian images and
feminist criticism are considered taboo in most Chicano theatres.

spheres as not "socially relevant" to Chicanos and typically not sanctioned in the Mexican household. These issues included female sexuality generally and male homosexuality and lesbianism specifically, as well as incest and violence against women—all of which are still relevant between the sheets and within the walls of many Chicano families. In the process, the Chicano Movement forfeited the participation and vision of some very significant female and gay leaders and never achieved the kind of harmonious Chicano "familia" they ostensibly sought.

To this day, although lip service is given to "gender issues" in academic and political circles, no serious examination of male supremacy within the Chicano community has taken place among heterosexual men. Veteranos of Chicano nationalism are some of the worst offenders. Twenty years later, they move into "elderhood" without having seriously grappled with the fact that their leadership in El Movimiento was made possible by all those women who kept their "plumas planchadas"[*] at every political event.

.....

A Divided Nation: A Chicana Lésbica Critique

We are free and sovereign to determine those tasks which are justly called for by our house, our land, the sweat of our brows, and by our hearts.

[*]The image alludes to Chicano cultural nationalists who during the seventies neoindigenist period sometimes wore feathers (plumas) and other Indian attire at cultural events.

*Aztlán belongs to those who plant the seeds, water the fields, and gather
the crops and not to the foreign Europeans. We do not recognize capri-
cious frontiers on the bronze continent.*
—From "El Plan Espiritual de Aztlán"

When "El Plan Espiritual de Aztlán" was conceived a generation ago, lesbians and gay men were not envisioned as members of
the "house"; we were not recognized as the sister planting the seeds,
the brother gathering the crops. We were not counted as members
of the "bronze continent."

In the last decade, through the efforts of Chicana feministas,
Chicanismo has undergone a serious critique. Feminist critics are
committed to the preservation of Chicano culture, but we know that
our culture will not survive marital rape, battering, incest, drug and
alcohol abuse, AIDS, and the marginalization of lesbian daughters
and gay sons. Some of the most outspoken criticism of the Chicano
Movement's sexism and some of the most impassioned activism in
the area of *Chicana* liberation (including work on sexual abuse,
domestic violence, immigrant rights, Indigenous women's issues,
health care, etc.) have been advanced by lesbians.

Since lesbians and gay men have often been forced out of our
blood families, and since our love and sexual desire are not housed
within the traditional family, we are in a critical position to address
those areas within our cultural family that need to change. Further,
in order to understand and defend our lovers and our same-sex
loving, lesbians and gay men must come to terms with how homophobia, gender roles, and sexuality are learned and expressed in
Chicano culture. As Ricardo Bracho writes: "To speak of my desire,
to find voice in my brown flesh, I needed to confront my male mirror."
As a lesbian, I don't pretend to understand the intricacies or intima-

cies of Chicano gay desire, but we do share the fact that our "homosexuality"—our feelings about sex, sexual power and domination, feminity and masculinity, family, loyalty, and morality—has been shaped by heterosexist culture and society. As such, we have plenty to tell heterosexuals about themselves.

When we are moved sexually toward someone, there is a profound opportunity to observe the microcosm of all human relations, to understand power dynamics both obvious and subtle, and to meditate on the core creative impulse of all desire. Desire is never politically correct. In sex, gender roles, race relations, and our collective histories of oppression and human connection are enacted. Since the early 1980s, Chicana lesbian feminists have explored these traditionally "dangerous" topics in both critical and creative writings. Chicana lesbian-identified writers such as Ana Castillo, Gloria Anzaldúa, and Naomi Littlebear Moreno were among the first to articulate a Chicana feminism, which included a radical woman-centered critique of sexism *and sexuality* from which both lesbian and heterosexual women benefited.

In the last few years, Chicano gay men have also begun to openly examine Chicano sexuality. I suspect heterosexual Chicanos will have the world to learn from their gay brothers about their shared masculinity, but they will have the most to learn from the "queens," the "maricones." Because they are deemed "inferior" for not fulfilling the traditional role of men, they are more marginalized from mainstream heterosexual society than other gay men and are especially vulnerable to male violence. Over the years, I have been shocked to discover how many femme gay men have grown up regularly experiencing rape and sexual abuse. The rapist is always heterosexual and usually Chicano like themselves. What has the Gay Movement done for these brothers? What has the Chicano

Movement done? What do these young and once-young men have to tell us about misogyny and male violence? Like women, they see the macho's desire to dominate the feminine, but even more intimately because they both desire men and share manhood with their oppressor. They may be jotos, but they are still men, and are bound by their racial and sexual identification to men (Bracho's "male mirror").

Until recently, Chicano gay men have been silent over the Chicano Movement's male heterosexual hegemony. As much as I see a potential alliance with gay men in our shared experience of homophobia, the majority of gay men still cling to what privileges they can. I have often been severely disappointed and hurt by the misogyny of gay Chicanos. Separation from one's brothers is a painful thing. Being gay does not preclude gay men from harboring the same sexism evident in heterosexual men. It's like white people and racism, sexism goes with the (male) territory.

On some level, our brothers—gay and straight—have got to give up being "men." I don't mean give up their genitals, their unique expression of desire, or the rich and intimate manner in which men can bond together. Men have to give up their subscription to male superiority. I remember during the Civil Rights Movement seeing newsreel footage of young Black men carrying protest signs reading "I AM A MAN." It was a powerful statement, publicly declaring their humanness in a society that daily told them otherwise. But they didn't write "I AM HUMAN," they wrote "MAN." Conceiving of their liberation in male terms, they were unwittingly demanding the right to share the whiteman's position of male dominance. This demand would become consciously articulated with the emergence of the male-dominated Black Nationalist Movement. The liberation of Black women per se was not part of the program, except to the extent that better conditions for the race in general might benefit Black women as well.

How differently Sojourner Truth's "Ain't I a Woman" speech resonates for me. Unable to choose between suffrage and abolition, between her womanhood and her Blackness, Truth's 19th-century call for a free Black womanhood in a Black- and woman-hating society required the freedom of all enslaved and disenfranchised peoples. As the Black feminist Combahee River Collective stated in 1977, "If Black women were free, it would mean that everyone else would have to be free since our freedom would necessitate the destruction of all the systems of oppression." No progressive movement can succeed while any member of the population remains in submission.

Chicano gay men have been reluctant to recognize and acknowledge that their freedom is intricately connected to the freedom of women. As long as they insist on remaining "men" in the socially and culturally constructed sense of the word, they will never achieve the full liberation they desire. There will always be jotos getting raped and beaten. Within people of color communities, violence against women, gay bashing, sterilization abuse, AIDS and AIDS discrimination, gay substance abuse, and gay teen suicide emerge from the same source—a racist and mysogynist social and economic system that dominates, punishes, and abuses all things colored, female, or perceived as female-like. By openly confronting Chicano sexuality and sexism, gay men can do their own part to unravel how both men *and* women have been formed and deformed by racist Amerika and our misogynist/catholic/colonized mechicanidad; and we can come that much closer to healing those fissures that have divided us as a people.

The AIDS epidemic has seriously shaken the foundation of the Chicano gay community, and gay men seem more willing than ever to explore those areas of political change that will ensure their survival. In their fight against AIDS, they have been rejected and neglected by both the white gay male establishment and the Latino heterosexual health-care community. They also have witnessed direct support by Latina lesbians.[*] Unlike the "queens" who have always been open about their sexuality, "passing" gay men have learned in a visceral way that being in "the closet" and preserving their "manly" image will not protect them, it will only make their dying more secret. I remember my friend Arturo Islas, the novelist. I think of how his writing begged to boldly announce his gayness. Instead, we learned it through vague references about "sinners" and tortured alcoholic characters who wanted nothing more than to "die dancing" beneath a lightning-charged sky just before a thunderstorm. Islas died of AIDS-related illness in 1990, having barely begun to examine the complexity of Chicano sexuality in his writing. I also think of essayist Richard Rodríguez, who, with so much death surrounding him, has recently begun to publicly address the subject of homosexuality; and yet, even ten years ago we all knew "Mr. Secrets" was gay from his assimilationist *Hunger of Memory*.^{**} Had he "come out" in 1982, the white establishment would have been far less willing to promote him as the "Hispanic" anti-affirmative action spokesperson. He would have lost a lot of validity...and opportunity. But how many lives are lost each time

---

* In contrast to the overwhelming response by lesbians to the AIDS crisis, breast cancer, which has disproportionately affected the lesbian community, has received little attention from the gay men's community in particular, and the public at large. And yet, the statistics are devastating. One out of every nine women in the United States will get breast cancer: 44,500 U.S. women will die of breast cancer this year (*Boston Globe*, November 5, 1991).

**See Rodríguez' essay "Late Victorians" in his most recent collection, *Days of Obligation: An Argument with My Mexican Father*.

we cling to privileges that make other people's lives more vulnerable
to violence?

At this point in history, lesbians and gay men can make a
significant contribution to the creation of a new Chicano movement,
one passionately committed to saving lives. As we are forced to
struggle for our right to love free of disease and discrimination,
"Aztlán" as our imagined homeland begins to take on renewed
importance. Without the dream of a free world, a free world will
never be realized. Chicana lesbians and gay men do not merely seek
inclusion in the Chicano nation; we seek a nation strong enough to
embrace a full range of racial diversities, human sexualities, and
expressions of gender. We seek a culture that can allow for the
natural expression of our femaleness and maleness and our love
without prejudice or punishment. In a "queer" Aztlán, there would
be no freaks, no "others" to point one's finger at.   My Native
American friends tell me that in some Native American tribes, gay
men and lesbians were traditionally regarded as "two-spirited"
people. Displaying both masculine and feminine aspects, they were
highly respected members of their community, and were thought to
possess a higher spiritual development.[*] Hearing of such traditions
gives historical validation for what Chicana lesbians and gay men
have always recognized—that lesbians and gay men play a significant spiritual, cultural, and political role within the Chicano community.   Somos activistas, académicos y artistas, parteras y

---

[*] This was not the case among all tribes nor is homosexuality generally
condoned in contemporary Indian societies. See "Must We Deracinate
Indians to Find Gay Roots?" by Ramón A. Gutiérrez in *Outlook: National Lesbian and Gay Quarterly,* Winter 1989.

políticos, curanderas y campesinos. With or without heterosexual acknowledgement, lesbians and gay men have continued to actively redefine familia, cultura, and comunidad. We have formed circles of support and survival, often drawing from the more egalitarian models of Indigenous communities.

.....

Indigenismo: The Re-tribalization of Our People

In recent years, for gay and straight Chicanos alike, our indigenismo has increased in importance as we witness the ultimate failure of Anglo-Americanism to bring harmony to our lives. In Ward Churchill's *Struggle for the Land,* he describes an "Indigenist" as someone who "takes the rights of indigenous peoples as the highest priority," and who "draws upon the traditions...of native peoples the world over." Many Chicanos would by this definition consider themselves Indigenists, subscribing to an indigenismo that is derived specifically from the traditions of mechicano indio peoples. Since the early seventies, Chicanos have worked in coalition with other Native American tribes and have participated in inter-tribal gatherings, political-prisoner campaigns, land-rights struggles, and religious ceremonies. Chicano Nation has been varyingly accepted as a tribe by other Native American peoples, usually more in the honorary sense than in any official capacity. The Indigenous Women's Network, for example, has included Chicanas since its inception in 1984.

Most Chicanos can claim, through physical traits alone, that we are of Native blood (we often joke that Chicanos are usually the

most Indian-looking people in a room full of "skins"). The majority
of us, however, has been denied direct information regarding our
tribal affiliations. Since our origins are usually in the Southwest and
México, Chicanos' Indian roots encompass a range of nations including Apache, Yaqui, Papago, Navajo, and Tarahumara from the
border regions, as well as dozens of Native tribes throughout
México. Regardless of verifiable genealogy, many Chicanos have
recently begun to experience a kind of collective longing to return to
our culture's traditional Indigenous beliefs and ways of constructing
community in order to find concrete solutions for the myriad prob-
lems confronting us, from the toxic dump sites in our neighborhoods
to rape.

"Tribe," based on the traditional models of Native Americans,
is an alternative socioeconomic structure that holds considerable
appeal for those of us who recognize the weaknesses of the isolated
patriarchal capitalist family structure. This is not to say that all
Native Americans subscribe to the same tribal structures or that
contemporary Indians fully practice traditional tribal ways. Few
Native peoples today are allowed real political autonomy and self-
determination. Tribal governments are corrupted by U.S. interfer-
ence through the Bureau of Indian Affairs, the U.S. military, the
F.B.I., and the U.S. Department of Energy. In essence, however, the
tribal model is a form of community-building that can accommodate
socialism, feminism, and environmental protection. In an ideal
world, tribal members are responsive and responsible to one another
and the natural environment. Cooperation is rewarded over com-
petition. Acts of violence against women and children do not occur
in secret and perpetrators are held accountable to the rest of the
community. "Familia" is not dependent upon male-dominance or

heterosexual coupling. Elders are respected and women's leadership is fostered, not feared.

But it is not an ideal world. Any Indian on or off the reservation can tell you about the obstacles to following traditional ways. The reservation is not indigenous to Native Americans; it is a colonial model invented to disempower Native peoples. The rates of alcoholism, suicide, and domestic violence are testimony to the effectiveness of that system. Chicanos, living in the colony of the U.S. barrio, have the same scars: AIDS, drugs, brown-on-brown murder, poverty, and environmental contamination. Nevertheless, the present-day values and organized struggles of traditional Native communities throughout the Americas represent real hope for halting the quickly accelerating level of destruction affecting all life on this continent.

.....

Madre Tierra / Madre Mujer: The Struggle for Land[*]

Journal Entry

I sit in a hotel room. A fancy hotel room with two walls of pure glass and pure Vancouver night skyline filling them. I sit on top of the

[*]I wish to thank Marsha Gómez, the Indigenous Women's Network, and the Alma de Mujer Center for Social Change in Austin, Texas, for providing me with statistical and other current information about Indigenous peoples' struggles for environmental safety and sovereignty, as well as published materials on the '92 Earth Summit in Brazil.

bed and eat Japanese take-out. The Canadian t.v. news takes us east
to the province of Quebec, to some desolate area with no plumbing or
sewage, no running water, where a group of Inuit people have been
displaced. To some desolate area where Inuit children stick their faces
into bags and sniff gas fumes for the high, the rush, the trip, for the
escape out of this hell-hole that is their life. One young boy gives the
finger to the t.v. camera. "They're angry, " an Inuit leader states. "I'm
angry, too." At thirty, he is already an old man. And I hate this Canada
as much as I hate these dis-United States.

But I go on eating my Japanese meal that has somehow
turned rotten on my tongue and my bloody culpability mixes with
the texture of dead fish flesh and no wonder I stand on the very edge
of the balcony on the 26th floor of this hotel looking down on
restaurant-row Vancouver and imagine how easy and impossible it
would be to leap in protest for the gas-guzzling Inuit children.

.....

The primary struggle for Native peoples across the globe is the
struggle for land. In 1992, 500 years after the arrival of Columbus,
on the heels of the Gulf War and the dissolution of the Soviet Union,
the entire world is reconstructing itself. No longer frozen into the
Soviet/Yanqui paradigm of a "Cold" and invented "War," Indigenous
peoples are responding en masse to the threat of a global capitalist
"mono-culture" defended by the "hired guns" of the U.S. military.
Five hundred years after Columbus' arrival, they are spearheading
an international movement with the goal of sovereignty for all
Indigenous nations.

Increasingly, the struggles on this planet are not for "nation-
states," but for nations of people, bound together by spirit, land,

language, history, and blood.* This is evident from the intifada of the Palestinians residing within Israel's stolen borders and the resistance of the Cree and Inuit Indians in northern Quebec. The Kurds of the Persian Gulf region understand this, as do the Ukrainians of what was once the Soviet Union. Chicanos are also a nation of people, internally colonized within the borders of the U.S. nation-state.

Few Chicanos really believe we can wrest Aztlán away from Anglo-America. And yet, residing in those Southwestern territories, especially those areas not completely appropriated by gringolandia, we instinctively remember it as Mexican Indian land and can still imagine it as a distinct nation. In our most private moments, we ask ourselves, *If the Soviet Union could dissolve, why can't the United States?*

Dreams of the disintegration of the United States as we know it are not so private among North American Indians. The dissolution of the Soviet Union has given renewed impetus to seccessionist thinking by Indians here in the United States. One plan, the "North American Union of Indigenous Nations," described in Ward Churchill's book, calls for the reunification of Indian peoples and territories to comprise a full third of continental United States, including much of Aztlán. Not surprisingly, Chicano Nation is not

*The dissolution of what was heretofore the nation-state of Yugoslavia, composed of Serbs, Slovenes, Croats, Albanians, and Macedonians, including the Muslim and Orthodox religions, represents the rise of bitter nationalist sentiment gone awry. It is a horror story of ethnic and cultural nationalism turned into nazism and serves as a painful warning against fascist extremism in nationalist campaigns.

mentioned as part of this new confederacy, which speaks to the still tenuous alliance between Chicano and Native American peoples. Nevertheless, the spirit of the plan is very much in accord with Chicano nationalists' most revolutionary dreams of reclaiming a homeland, side by side with other Indian Nations.

.....

If the material basis of every nationalist movement is land, then the reacquisition, defense, and protection of Native land and its natural resources are the basis for rebuilding Chicano nation. Without the sovereignty of Native peoples, including Chicanos, and support for our land-based struggles, the world will be lost to North American greed, and our culturas lost with it. The "last frontier" for Northern capitalists lies buried in coal-and uranium-rich reservation lands and in the remaining rainforests of the Amazon. The inhabitants of these territories—the Diné, the North Cheyenne, the Kayapó, etc.—are the very people who in 1992 offer the world community "living models" of ways to live in balance with nature and safeguard the earth as we know it. The great historical irony is that 500 years after the Conquest, the conqueror must now turn to the conquered for salvation.

We are speaking of bottom-line considerations. I can't understand when in 1992 with 100 acres of rainforest disappearing every minute, with global warming, with babies being born without brains in South Tejas, with street kids in Río sniffing glue to stifle their hunger, with Mohawk women's breast milk being contaminated by the poisoned waters of the Great Lakes Basin, how we as people of color, as people of Indian blood, as people with the same last names as our Latin American counterparts, are not alarmed by the destruc-

tion of Indigenous and mestizo peoples. How is it Chicanos cannot
see ourselves as victims of the same destruction, already in its
advanced stages? Why do we not collectively experience the urgency
for alternatives based not on what our oppressors advise, but on the
advice of elders and ancestors who may now speak to us only in
dreams?

What they are telling us is very clear. The road to the future
is the road from our past. Traditional Indigenous communities (our
Indian "past" that too many Chicanos have rejected) provide prac-
tical answers for our survival. At the Earth Summit in Río de Janeiro
in June 1992, representatives from "developing countries," and
grassroots, Indigenous, and people-of-color organizations joined together to demand the economic programs necessary to create their
own sustainable ecologically-sound communities. In a world where
eighty-five percent of all the income, largely generated from the
natural resources of Indigenous lands and "Third World" countries,
goes to twenty-three percent of the people, Fidel Castro said it best:
"Let the ecological debt be paid, not the foreign debt."

And here all the connecting concerns begin to coalesce. Here
the Marxist meets the ecologist. We need look no further than the
North American Free Trade Agreement (NAFTA) to understand the
connection between global ecological devastation and the United
States' relentless drive to expand its markets. NAFTA is no more
than a 21st-century plot to continue the North's exploitation of the
cheap labor, lax environmental policies, and the natural resources
of the South. The United States has no intention of responding to
the environmental crisis. George Bush's decision to "stand alone on
principle" and refuse to sign the Bio-Diversity Treaty said it all.
Profit over people. Profit over protection. No sustainable development is possible in the Americas if the United States continues to

demand hamburgers, Chrysler automobiles, and refrigerators from hungry, barefoot, and energy-starved nations. There is simply not enough to go around, no new burial ground for toxic waste that isn't sacred, no untapped energy source that doesn't suck the earth dry. Except for the sun...except for the wind, which are infinite in their generosity and virtually ignored.

.....

The earth is female. Whether myth, metaphor, or memory, she is called "Mother" by all peoples of all times. *Madre Tierra.* Like woman, Madre Tierra has been raped, exploited for her resources, rendered inert, passive, and speechless. Her cries manifested in earthquakes, tidal waves, hurricanes, volcanic eruptions are not heeded. But the Indians take note and so do the women, the women with the capacity to remember.

Native religions have traditionally honored the female alongside the male. Religions that grow exclusively from the patriarchal capitalist imagination, instead of the requirements of nature, enslave the female body. The only religion we need is one based on the good sense of living in harmony with nature. Religion should serve as a justification against greed, not for it. Bring back the rain gods, corn gods, father sun, and mother moon and keep those gods happy. Whether we recognize it or not, those gods are today, this day, punishing us for our excess. What humankind has destroyed will wreak havoc on the destoyer. Fried skin from holes in the ozone is only one example.

The earth is female. It is no accident then that the main grassroots activists defending the earth, along with Native peoples, are women of all races and cultures. Regardless of the so-called "advances" of Western "civilization," women remain the chief care-takers, nurturers, and providers for our children and our elders. These are the mothers of East Los Angeles, McFarland, and Kettleman City, fighting toxic dumps, local incinerators and pesticide poisoning, women who experience the earth's contamination in the deformation and death occurring within their very wombs. We do not have to be mothers to know this. Most women know what it is to be seen as the Earth is seen—a receptacle for male violence and greed. Over half the agricultural workers in the world are women who receive less training and less protection than their male counterparts. We do not control how we produce and reproduce, how we labor and love. And *how will our lands be free if our bodies aren't?*

Land remains the common ground for all radical action. But land is more than the rocks and trees, the animal and plant life that make up the territory of Aztlán or Navajo Nation or Maya Mesoamerica. For immigrant and native alike, land is also the factories where we work, the water our children drink, and the housing project where we live. For women, lesbians, and gay men, land is that physical mass called our bodies. Throughout las Américas, all these "lands" remain under occupation by an Anglo-centric, patriarchal, imperialist United States.

.....

La Causa Chicana: Entering the Next Millennium

As a Chicana lesbian, I know that the struggle I share with all Chicanos and Indigenous peoples is truly one of sovereignty, the sovereign right to wholly inhabit oneself (*cuerpo y alma*) and one's territory (*pan y tierra*). I don't know if we can ever take back Aztlán from Anglo-America, but in the name of a new Chicano nationalism we can work to defend remaining Indian territories. We can work to teach one another that our freedom as a people is mutually dependent and cannot be parceled out—class before race before sex before sexuality. A new Chicano nationalism calls for the integration of both the traditional and the revolutionary, the ancient and the contemporary. It requires a serious reckoning with the weaknesses in our mestizo culture, and a reaffirmation of what has preserved and sustained us as a people. I am clear about one thing: fear has not sustained us. Fear of action, fear of speaking, fear of women, fear of queers.

As these 500 years come to a close, I look forward to a new América, where the only "discovery" to be made is the rediscovery of ourselves as members of the global community. Nature will be our teacher, for she alone knows no prejudice. Possibly as we ask men to give up being "men," we must ask humans to give up being "human," or at least to give up the human capacity for greed. Simply, we must give back to the earth what we take from it. We must submit to a higher "natural" authority, as we invent new ways of making culture, making tribe, to survive and flourish as members of the world community in the next millennium.

Tribute

to Rodrigo Reyes[*]

the death of a brother
a sudden glimpsed brother
an estranged brother
a once touched brother...

Last night at the service, I kept thinking...Rodrigo loved his own kind, his own brown and male kind. Listening to the tributes

[*] Rodrigo Reyes was a community organizer, theatre director, actor, poet, and painter who made his life in the Gay Latino Mission District of San Francisco. He died of AIDS-related illness on January 19, 1992.

made to him, it was clear that the hearts he touched the most deeply were his carnalitos. And each one, as lovely as the one preceding him, spoke about Rodrigo, "mi 'mano, mi papito, mi carnal, ese cabrón…" con un cariño wholly felt.

For a moment, I wondered if women had ever entered his heart in the same way. Perhaps, his mother did when once as a young teenager, he told her, "Déjalo," referring to his father. "Leave him, amá. Yo te cuido. We don't need him." When Rodrigo told me that story from his sickbed, a different Rodrigo came into view, a man who was once a boy with a boy's earnestness to protect and defend his mother, with a boy's desire to conceive of a manhood outside of abuso. We were all inocentes once and we carry that broken innocence into every meeting of every stranger, every potential amante.

Was it in the same visit he asked me, the barriers between us momentarily dissolving, as we met eye to eye, artist to artist, "Do you see that painting?" pointing to a living mass of color on the wall. "Yes," I answered. "That painting just passed through me," he said. "Rodrigo didn't paint that, it just happened. Rodrigo disappeared. Do you understand?" And a desire welled up in me, to meet this man, to finally speak with a brother about my most private place, that place where the work possesses us and our pitiful egos take flight. "Yes," I answer. "I understand." He told me that all he wanted was a little more time, a little more time to repeat that moment, to be the servant of his art, and utterly humbled in the creation of it. There *is* no greater joy. And how I wanted him to live, too…for just that reason.

The gift of the dying is that they allow us to contemplate our own deaths, our own meanings…our own creations. I thank him for this.

Me, with some time still to spare. This is the gift Rodrigo offers to all of us who survive him.

I wonder why and how we live in an era when dying is such a visceral part of our daily lives. Possibly, living in San Francisco and not San Salvador, we imagined we would be spared such a relentlessly intimate acquaintance with death, an intimacy seldom experienced except in times of war and natural disaster; but this is the era in which we live. Women dying in droves from cancer; gay men/colored folk dying of AIDS. I don't know what to make of it. It has barely begun to touch my life. Perhaps I have Rodrigo to thank again for this—initiating me to life with the knowledge of death.

Last night the homage given to Rodrigo convinced me how rare it is to be colored and queer and live to speak about it. In honoring Rodrigo, one young man said, "Rodrigo devoted his entire life to the community." And I would like to add, and he devoted his entire passion to his own brown brothers. He delighted in their beauty, their desire, and their hope. He wanted them to be free, and righteously. I believe that in Rodrigo's final months and in his final words, he saw a much clearer road toward that freedom, and that it had something to do with the freedom of women, too. I believe he started to understand this, not in his head, but in his gut, when he looked upon so much death and drugs and despair within his own community.

The last thing I did for Rodrigo, the last time I saw him, was cut his toenails. I marveled at it, how after all our heated debates, it had come down to this simple act. He was my brother, after all, and he needed his toenails cut. I confess, I did not always feel recognized by Rodrigo as a sister. At times I felt that the sisters simply didn't matter to him. And in each rejection I saw the face of my own blood brother. Let us not kid ourselves, this *is* what we bring to our meetings as latinos, lesbianas, jotos, políticas—all the wounds of family betrayals and abandonments. But I know—with or without his recognition—that (as artists and queers) we were intimately tied to each other's survival, knowledge, y libertad.

He did make space for them, his brothers
he did plant seeds,
he did lay ground.
And this is where the young ones pick up...

¡Adelante 'manitos!

— January 23, 1992

Where Beauty Resides

Maya mathematics from the beginning of the Classic Period in-cluded...the concept of zero, principally as a symbol of completeness.
                                        — Miguel León Portilla

1

Your hand, a cup
that empties me
of myself.
I am reduced
to zero.
I meditate on how I will live
without reflection.

The quiet invades.

Thursday morning and minutes ago you were here with me.
I look out onto a city of grey and steel blue structures
I spot you folded into one of them
red brick lining the walls where you work
you are thinking of me
you put pencil to your lip
teeth imbedded into knuckle
you inhale
what was once me or the scent of your own
expectant
desire.

Here, indoors, the city is not grey
the sheets are a steel blue that ignite your eyes
searching me strip searching me,
I have gone no more
your hand has only emptied me of all want.
"Satisfecha," I say the word hard like sex
whole in meaning.

When you rise I watch you
cover your body
your elbows spread like crooked wings
bra snaps behind your back
you step into panties
sliding up thighs
your wound mouth disappears
shirt slipping over head
you emerge, a radiant medusa.

I see you as I was instructed to,
"you have a beautiful body"
you smile, snap up the crotch
of your jeans...
but your beauty resides elsewhere
you know this too
emptied of ourselves.

.....

I only ask this one thing of you:
Beyond woman hidden in woman

resides child hidden in child
resides zero.

There is no loneliness there
but a strangeness, I admit
my eyes scanning the cityscape for your shape
against the fog's haze, I search
strip search these words
emptied of myself.

2
"A cup is molded of clay
but its...hollow space
is the useful part."*

As a catholic schoolgirl I would have confessed
the sin of you   my body, a temple
the temple of my undoing.

I suspect this feeling is called sadness
I suspect I used to name this loneliness
your back walking out the door
the weight of another being as fragile
as delicate as lonely as mine
heavy upon your shoulders.

* Carolyn Merchant, *Radical Ecology: The Search for a Livable World.*

I think of others, too, while I kiss you,
pacts we make in the stolen hours of urban life.
I'll promise you anything
for the bowl of your breasts and thighs
to contain me once more this morning this bed.

I am speaking of something else here
with no name
it is about the number zero
without loneliness betrayal regret
you emptied me of myself.

.....

When you leave, what I remember as fear
a vague sense of relief
a panicked moment of abandonment
what I remember in myriad
faces of lovers at myriad
numbers of doors in myriad
faceless numberless cities
dissipates from me
I watch you leave emptied of those memories
I watch you leave and enter me
my eyes, liquid
prey before her hunter.

Return to me, amor, again
and again with the same animal hunger.

I will not refuse you I have nothing left to lose.
You cannot devour what is infinite you drink
until replenished and drink again
and I am the receiver of your thirst
your tongue, my blessing
your hands, gifts from the gods.

I am emptied of myself.
Relieved of this burden.
My body a sacrament,
a flame
a holy sacrifice.

All else is blasphemy.

3
I am writing you to reach you without words
you will not read these words as much as you will see them
this day written in the bay grey sky
you will know me better than you imagined
forgive me everything
and the generosity will lay upon us
span the bridge that links and divides us

and I could go on writing like this forever
only guessing
at what lies inside
the shape and size of these letters.

Codex Xerí: El Momento Histórico

*Amid the fires of the Los Angeles Rebellion, on the eve of a fading Quinto
Sol and a rising new época, I paint in scribe colors—the black of this ink,
the red of those fires—my own Chicano codex. I offer it as a
closing prayer for the last generation.*

Picture this. It is May 1, 1992. Fifty-eight people are dead,
hundreds injured, and thousands are arrested across the country.
In my hometown of San Francisco, the mayor calls a state of
emergency. Young people—brown, black, white—are rounded up.
Anyone walking the streets of the barrio after seven pm is arrested:
hundreds of protesters spilling out of Dolores Park, two women who
happen to be coming home from a nearby wedding, another risking

an emergency trip to the store (any store she can find open) to buy tampons. Hours later, she's in the Santa Rita jail, still bleeding.

.....

After these Roman hieroglyphs have been pressed onto the printed page, history will have advanced well beyond the time of this writing; but as the Maya understood, a date is not a beginning, but the culmination of history in all its totality. What we are witnessing today took 500 years of conquest to create.[*]

It is 1992 and Los Angeles is on fire. Half a millennium after the arrival of Columbus, the Mesoamerican prophecies are being fulfilled. The enslaved have taken to the streets, burning down the conqueror's golden cities. A decade-long plague that attacks the very immune system upon which our survival depends assumes pandemic proportions. There is famine and worldwide dislocation.

[*]This essay was originally written for the Mexican Museum's 1992 "Chicano Codices Encountering Art of the Américas," curated by Marcos Sánchez-Tranquilino. Representing twenty-five Chicano artists from across the United States, the exhibit's task was to create a contemporary response to the Mesoamerican codices, the pictorial record books of Indigenous American thought largely destroyed by the fires of the Spanish conquest. Much of the visual imagery incorporated in this essay was inspired by codices by Amalia Mesa-Bains, Barbara Carrasco, Emanuel Martínez, Emmanuel Catarino Montoya, Delilah Montoya, the East Los Streetscapers, Carmen Lomas Garza, Willie Herrón, Kathy Vargas, Marcos Raya, Marta Sánchez, Lawrence Yáñez, and Celia Herrera Rodríguez.

People are living in refrigerator boxes on the streets of Aztlán. Earthquakes jolt the California coastline with increasing regularity. And with such violent movement, our ancient codices have predicted, this era—"El Quinto Sol"—will be destroyed. The temple has been toppled and is falling into flames. This is the American destiny. *There are dark patches on the faces of the children. They are crying.*

.....

It was not always like this.

In the beginning there were no contradictions. God, Ometeotl, the origin of all life, was both woman and man, Omecihuatl and Ometecuhtli. The paradox of our native existence—that we both govern our fate and are predetermined to live it—was no more than a naked truth depicted in a poem, a song, an embroidered mantle, a jaguar god etched into jadeite. Science was less intelligent than art. And art and its makers were respected. Metaphor expressed what the intellect suffered: la flor de nuestro ser, su belleza, su fragilidad. Her temporal and fleeting essence.

Five hundred years later, our deepest memories are mere colorless glimpses: paper cut-outs of the ancient dalia, maguey, lagartija. Our reptilian regeneration lies fragmented, hand split from heart. Decapitated, our speech scrolled tongues float in a wordless sea. *How did we grow so speechless?*

We know the red path. Bloody footprints on urban streetscapes. We assimilated, put on the white mask. We have been sleepwalking the road of "Davy Crockett" heroes.

7
The Chicano codex is the map back to the original face. Its scribes are the modern-day tlamatinime. We grab our raza's face and turn it in our palm. We hold up the obsidian mirror, tell them, "Look, gente, so that you might know yourselves, find your true face and heart, and see."

The Chicano codex es una peregrinación to an América unwritten. América: the brown swell of tierra indígena debajo de la Calavera. Our rapist wears the face of death. In a suit of armor, he rides us—cross in one hand, sword in the other. And this is how they've always taken us with their gods of war and their men of god. The Chicano codex is a demand for retribution—retribution for land and lives lost. Our records show the sum of Chicano existence engraved on tombstones: World War I, World War II, Korea, Vietnam, Iraq. Our records show a five-century-long list of tributes paid to illegal landlords. We want it *all* back, Señor, starting with California, Nevada, Arizona, Tejas, Nuevo México...

> *Keep those "40 pieces of gold the size of communion hosts," and give us back Colorado, Cabrón. Keep your small-pox infested blankets, syphilis-infected Spaniards, and give us back the Taínos. Keep your Cortez and give us back Peltier. Return the rain forests and we'll return genocide, alcoholism, drug addiction, and nuclear disaster.*

Chicano scribes are deconstructing the gringo history of greed. The real history kept from us, we scratch it on barrio walls, deciphering modern-day hieroglyphs—pachuco slang blending into urban guerrillero tongue, "U.S. out of Aztlán NOW!" "Cada marca escarbando el rostro de nuestra memoria."[*] And there in the Mar Vista Gardens on the stoneface of a housing project, a heart is drawn in the shape of a breast. Can you see it? The soft arc of vulva. There. The backbone of a woman winding into a Quetzalcóatl mind. And the women whisper:

> *we are more than*
> *mujer before metate*
> *we are more than*
> *mujer before metate*
> *we are more...*

A Mechicana glyph. Con Safos.

.....

How many corn cakes a day do the children of Aztlán need to survive?

The Chicano codex is a portrait of our daily lives. Images of spam next to a stack of store-bought tortillas. Chavalitos working

---

[*] From the notes for Codex Zelia by Celia Herrera Rodríguez.

in the family panadería. We are a codex of lotería and boxing matches. We pick nopales, graduate from college, are elected County Supervisor. We low-ride in East Los, bumper to bumper in minitrucks. We light candles at La Placita. *For whom do we pray?*

In the circle of this oración we form a contemporary urban Chicano glyph. A small group of jotería, "two-spirited" people, standing in the shadow de Los Pechos de La India (San Francisco). Two lush green mounds of female protection. A radio tower piercing her breast.

We sprinkle his ashes in the comadre's yard, an urban jardín of coffee-can pots and desert succulents. It's a wonder how the Mexican desert survives here under the ever-damp serape of bay fog. We fill the mouth of each can with the white dust of his bones, una cucharita at a time. Sea birds pass overhead. One woman announces. "Miren, there goes our brother. See how without flesh, he is free to fly." There is a small dog bearing witness. Y todavía we remember ceremony.

Our codices are a record of remembering. At times, we can only sense those memories intuitively like an "internal feather"—always present, always hidden, yet glowing iridescent under a Tejano full moon. Our memory is the umbilical cord buried beneath the shade of cottonwoods, where abuelita cuentos pour scroll-like from the tongue. It is the knowledge of aloe vera for sunburn, nopalitos for lonche, yerbabuena for just about anything.

Today, before writing, I burn the sage Juan brought back from the hills outside Tijuana. I plant the geraniums that Carmen gave me from her garden. I light a vela before la Virgen. And on christmas, Las

Comadres will put down our paintbrushes, turn off our computers, and stick our hands into the masa como han hecho las abuelas por siglos.

> *In these simple acts, we remember the forgotten,*
> *the fragmented,*
> *the dismembered.*
> *We re-member*
> *the severed serpent.*
>
> *We feed the dust of our bones to the plantas.*
> *And once again fertility is possible.*

The Chicano scribe remembers, not out of nostalgia but out of hope. She remembers in order to envision. She looks backward in order to look forward to a world founded not on greed, but on respect for the sovereignty of nature. And in this, she suffers—to know that fertility is both possible and constantly interrupted.

As it was for the tlamatinime centuries ago, the scribe's task is to interpret the signs of the time, read the writing on barrio walls, decode the hieroglyphs of street violence, unravel the skewed message of brown-on-brown crime and sister-rape. The Chicano codex is *our* book of revelation. It is the philosopher's stone, serpentine and regenerative. It prescribes our fate and releases us from it. It understands the relationship between darkness and dawn. *"Mira que te has de morir. Mira que no sabes cuándo."* [*]

.....

This Fifth Sun is quickly vanishing. Urban Warriors emerge on L.A. streetscapes. "Every empire falls," says the homeboy. "The Romans fell. The Egyptians fell. [The Aztecs fell]. This empire's gonna go, too." He, too, reads the writing on the wall. Five hundred years ago, our original colonizers came in search of Gold. And today, in Los Angeles and San Francisco our babies are being buried under it.

GOLD that's a Whirlpool dryer
GOLD that's a case of Pepsi Cola
GOLD that's a SONY television/VCR unit
GOLD that's AMERICAN EXPRESS CARD **GOLD**

And even this will not be sign enough.
Even this will not.

Each uprising es un paso en la jornada, the red path to baptism con la Madre Mescalera. Each action, another feather surfacing. It splits the chest, the skin bleeds. The planet is Crow Woman in whose mountain-breasts the missiles of destruction have been implanted.

* From Codex Amalia by Amalia Mesa-Bains.

We must open the wound to make it heal, purify ourselves with the prick of Maguey thorns. This Sun will not pass away painlessly!

It is 1992, and we are witnessing a new breed of revolucionario, their speech scrolls are slave tongues unraveling. Feathers in full plumage, they burn down the Alamo, Macy's San Francisco, the savings and loan, and every liquor store in South Central Los Angeles!

Meanwhile, Tlaliyolo—"corazón de la tierra"—prepares to turn over.

And we, the Codex-Makers, remove the white mask.
We wait and watch the horizon.

Our Olmeca third eye
begins to glisten
in the slowly
rising
light.

Sources Cited

Anzaldúa, Gloria. *Borderlands / La Frontera: The New Mestiza*. San Francisco: Spinsters/Aunt Lute Press, 1987.

—, and Moraga, Cherríe, eds. "The Combahee River Collective Statement." *This Bridge Called My Back: Writings by Radical Women of Color*. New York: Kitchen Table Press, 1983.

Bracho, Ricardo. "Sexual Sovereignty: Towards an Erotic of Chicano Liberation" and "Refracting Voices: Race, Gender, Desire." *The Alphabet Isn't Sopa*. Unpublished manuscript.

Castillo, Ana. *The Mixquihuala Letters*. Tempe, Arizona: Bilingual Press/Editorial bilingüe, 1986.

Cervantes, Lorna Dee. *Emplumada*. Pittsburgh: University of Pittsburgh Press, 1981.

Codex Mendoza: Aztec Manuscript. Commentary by Kurt Ross. London: Regent Books/High Text Ltd., 1984.

Fernández, Adela. *Dioses prehispánicos de México: Mitos y deidades del panteón náhuatl*. Mexico City: Panorama Editorial, 1989.

Gutiérrez, Ramón A. "Must We Deracinate Indians to Find Gay Roots?" *Outlook: National Lesbian and Gay Quarterly*, Winter 1989.

Instituto Nacional de Antropología e Historia. *Los Códices de México*. Mexico City, 1979.

Islas, Arturo. *Migrant Souls: A Novel*. New York: Morrow, 1990.

—*The Rain God: A Desert Tale*. Palo Alto: Alexandrian Press, 1984.

Léon-Portilla, Miguel. *Aztec Thought and Culture*. Norman, OK: University of Oklahoma Press, 1963.

Lorde, Audre. "Poetry Is Not a Luxury." *Sister Outsider: Essays & Speeches.* Trumansburg, NY: The Crossing Press, 1984.

Merchant, Carolyn. *Radical Ecology: The Search for a Livable World.* New York: Routledge, 1992.

Midnight Sun. "Sex/Gender Systems in Native North America." *Living the Spirit: A Gay American Indian Anthology.* Ed. Will Roscoe with Gay American Indians. New York: St. Martin's Press, 1988.

Morrison, Toni. *Sula.* New York: Knopf, 1974.

Nuttall, Zelia, ed. *The Codex Nuttall: A Picture Manuscript from Ancient Mexico.* New York: Dover Publications, 1975.

Pauli, Hertha Ernestine. *Her Name Was Sojourner Truth.* Pasadena: Appleton, 1962.

Pérez, Emma. "Sexuality and Discourse: Notes from a Chicana Survivor." *Chicana Lesbians: The Girls Our Mothers Warned Us About.* Ed. Carla Trujillo. Berkeley: Third Woman Press, 1991.

Pina, Michael. "The Archaic, Historical and Mythicized Dimension of Aztlán." *Aztlán: Essays on the Chicano Homeland,* eds. Rudolfo A. Anya and Francisco A. Lomelí. Albuquerque: Academia/El Norte Publications, 1989.

Rodríguez, Richard. *Days of Obligation: An Argument with My Mexican Father.* New York: Viking Press, 1992.

—*Hunger of Memory: The Education of Richard Rodríguez: An Autobiography.* Boston: D.R. Godine, 1982.

Shorris, Earl. *Latinos: A Biography of the People.* New York: Norton, 1992.

Steiner, Stan and Valdez, Luis, eds. "El Plan Espiritual de Aztlán." *Aztlán: An Anthology of Mexican American Literature.* New York: Vintage Books, 1972.

Thompson, William Irwin. *Blue Jade from the Morning Star: An Essay and a Cycle of Poems on Quetzalcoatl.* Hudson, NY: Lindisfarne Press, 1983.

Walker, Alice. "The Divided Life of Jean Toomer." *In Search of Our Mothers' Gardens.* New York: Harcourt Brace Jovanovich, 1983.

About the Author

Cherríe Moraga is a poet, playwright, and essayist. Some of her works include *Loving in the War Years, This Bridge Called My Back: Writings by Radical Women of Color, Shadow of a Man,* and *Heroes and Saints.* She has won numerous awards for her plays and poetry including the Before Columbus American Book Award, the Fund for New American Plays Award, and the National Endowment for the Arts Theatre Playwrights' Fellowship.

About South End Press

South End Press is a nonprofit, collectively run book publisher with over 180 titles in print. Since our founding in 1977, we have tried to meet the needs of readers who are exploring, or are already committed to, the politics of radical social change.

Our goal is to publish books that encourage critical thinking and constructive action on the key political, cultural, social, economic, and ecological issues shaping life in the United States and in the world. In this way, we hope to give expression to a wide diversity of democratic social movements and to provide an alternative to the products of corporate publishing.

If you would like a free catalog of South End Press books or information about our membership program—which offers two free books and a 40% discount on all titles—please write to us at South End Press, 116 Saint Botolph Street, Boston, MA 02115.

Other South End Press Titles of Interest

Loving in the War Years, Lo Que Nunca Pasó por Sus Labios
Cherríe Moraga

Sisters of the Yam, Black Women and Recovery
bell hooks

State of Native America, Genocide, Colonization and Resistance
edited by Annette Jaimes

Unsettling Relations,
The University as a Site of Feminist Struggles
Himani Bannerji, Linda Carty, Kari Dehli,
Susan Heald, and Kate McKenna